How to Negotiate Real Estate Contracts

For Buyers and Sellers

With Forms

By Mark Warda
Attorney at Law

SPHINX PUBLISHING
Sphinx International, Inc.
Post Office Box 25
1725 Clearwater/Largo Rd. S.
Clearwater, FL 34617
Tel: (813) 587-0999
Fax: (813) 586-5088

Note: The law changes constantly and is subject to different interpretations. It is up to you
to check it thoroughly before relying on it.
Neither the author nor the publisher guarantees the outcome of the uses to which this
material is put.

First Edition, 1993

ISBN 0-913825-59-X
Library of Congress Catalog Number 92-61841

Manufactured in the United States of America.

This publication is designed to provide accurate and authoritative information in regard to the
subject matter covered. It is sold with the understanding that the publisher is not engaged in
rendering legal, accounting or other professional services. If legal advice or other expert
assistance is required, the service of a competent professional person should be sought.

-From a Declaration of Principles jointly
adopted by a Committee of the American Bar
Association and a Committee of Publishers.

Published by Sphinx Publishing, a division of Sphinx International, Inc., Post Office Box 25,
Clearwater, Florida 34617-0025. This publication is available by mail for $14.95 plus $3.00
shipping plus Florida sales tax if applicable. For credit card orders call 1-800-226-5291.

Table of Contents

Introduction

No document is more important to a real estate transaction than the sales contract. All of the terms of the deal are controlled by the wording of the contract. The expenses at closing, the prorations, what property is included in the deal, as well as the price and payment terms are all decided when the contract is signed.

Many parties think the main concern when buying property is the price, but sophisticated buyers and sellers know that other terms can be even more important. With creative financing you can agree to pay tens of thousands of dollars more for a piece of property and actually save money in the long run. And with the right incentive you can buy property with little or no money down.

Unfortunately, most contracts are drafted on the first form found in the drawer, or on whatever the office supply store has in stock, or on the form provided by the seller's broker. Often a buyer pays thousands of dollars in extra expenses because he uses a form designed for a seller's benefit. Many times a seller gives more to a buyer than he intended simply because that is what the printed form said. Many people do not consult an attorney until after they have signed the contract! By then it is too late to improve the deal.

When buying or selling real property, you should keep in mind that there are in most cases no fixed rules as to who should pay for what. It doesn't matter that buyers *always* pay for the documentary stamps (or transfer tax) in your county. It doesn't matter that sellers *always* select their own title agent. It doesn't even matter that everywhere in the country taxes are prorated. Unless there is a specific law on the subject you are to free to make or accept any offer that suits you.

This book explains the different clauses found in real estate contracts and tells you which ones are best when you are buying or selling. Various versions of each clause are given so that you can choose the one most suitable to your deal. Some sample forms are provided covering a spectrum of needs. Most likely one of the forms will cover whatever deal you are putting together. To add additional clauses to them you can use the "Addendum" form provided in this book. On more complicated deals you may want to put together your own contract created from the clauses provided in this book.

Laws vary from state to state and some clauses in this book may not be allowed in certain areas. In some states an "approved contract" may be required. However, in many cases you can add your own terms with an addendum to the contract. Before using a contract you have drafted for yourself, you should have it reviewed by an experienced real estate attorney to be sure that it is legal and enforceable in your state and that it does what you intend it to do.

Chapter 1
Preparing Your Own Contract

While million-dollar deals are usually put together clause by clause, in most smaller deals people use whatever contract form is handy. Usually this is the form provided by the seller's real estate broker. While this often results in the buyer paying for things he could have avoided, it sometimes costs the seller money, too.

To make the best deal on any real estate purchase or sale you should be sure that every clause in your contract is in your best interest. Unfortunately, the high cost of lawyers' fees makes it financially prohibitive to have this done for many deals. This book is designed to help you understand the meaning of each clause in a real estate contract and how to use different clauses to make the best deal. Since most law schools today teach mainly theory, after reading this book you will know more about drafting real estate contracts than most law school graduates.

Using a Broker

Using a real estate broker can often save you a lot of money and time. An experienced broker will know what items in the contract can be negotiated and how to negotiate them. But occasionally a real estate broker will insist on using his own form in presenting an offer. This form will usually not be in your interest and will end up costing you thousands of dollars. Don't give in! Some brokers don't like new contract forms because they then have to read them. If they don't understand them they have to show them to their attorney and that will cost them money.

As mentioned elsewhere in this book, some states have laws requiring certain forms to be used. Some areas may have forms which have been "recommended" or "approved" by some group of lawyers or real estate agents. If a form is said to be required by law, be sure that this is the case. And if so, you will most likely be able to amend the terms with an addendum. If a form is merely "recommended" or "approved" by some group they can't force you to use it. In at least one case a contract drafted by a group of lawyers and real estate agents was held to be unenforceable.

A professional real estate agent will present all offers. If the one you are using refuses to present your offer on your contract, find a new agent. In some areas a real estate agent may be disciplined for refusing to present an offer.

As discussed in chapter 3, in many areas of the country there are real estate brokers working as "buyers' brokers" who only represent buyers of property. Buyers' brokers usually have their own contracts which are written in the interest of the buyer. These are much better than the forms provided by the seller's broker. However, they may not be as good as a contract you draft for yourself.

Even when working with a buyer's broker don't be afraid to suggest clauses you wish to add to the contract. Changing a few terms can save you thousands of dollars.

Printing Your Contract

You may be told that adding your clauses to a printed form contract will make them stand out and that they will not be accepted by the other party. One way to solve that is to have your contract typeset so that your terms are all part of the form. With desktop technology typesetting is cheap today and the cost should only be between $20 and $50 for a two page contract. This is nothing compared to what you can save by using this contract.

One investor had his own contract form printed up and put the words "Approved Form" at the top. When he presented it to sellers, often they, and even their attorneys, would look only at the terms typed in the blanks, and not read the fine print. Only when it came time for closing did they realize what horrible deals they had made.

Putting such a title at the top of your contract is not recommended since, if it ever went to court, it could be held to be false and misleading. But typesetting your clauses would make them look a lot more "standard" than typing them onto another contract.

Chapter 2
When to Use an Attorney

The purpose of this book is to provide legal information to you at a reasonable cost and to give you more control of your legal affairs. If you understand real estate contracts you can buy and sell property much more quickly and profitably than if you have to ask your attorney to look over everything you do.

Cost/Value Analysis

In deciding to rely on a $15 book rather than a $150-an-hour attorney you should make a cost/value analysis of the situation.

When buying a car you decide whether you want transportation, comfort, status or sex appeal, and you decide among such choices as a Chevette, a Lincoln, a Rolls Royce or a Porsche. Before making a decision you usually weigh the merits of each against the cost.

When you get a headache, you can take a pain reliever such as aspirin or you can go to a medical specialist for a neurological examination. Given this choice most people, of course, take a pain reliever, since it only costs pennies whereas a medical examination would cost hundreds of dollars and take a lot of time. This is usually a very logical choice because very rarely is anything more than a pain reliever needed for a headache. But in some cases a headache may indicate a brain tumor and failing to go to a specialist right away can result in complications. Should everyone with a headache go to a specialist? Of course not, but people treating their own illnesses must realize that they are taking a chance, based upon their cost/ value analysis of the situation, that they are taking the most logical option.

The same analysis should be done when deciding to buy or sell a piece of property. If you have owned several homes and successfully negotiated the purchase and sale of them without an attorney, and you are now buying another, you can probably handle it yourself (and use the information in this book to save thousands of dollars on the price.) But if you have always used an attorney or have never purchased property before and are now about to buy a 300-unit apartment complex, you should weigh the cost of using an attorney against what you could lose if you make a mistake.

One factor which will control your decision is the quality and experience of the attorneys you know. If the only attorneys you have used have been arrogant and obnoxious and billed you for much more than the value of the services they provided, then you will probably avoid them at all costs. But if you know a congenial attorney who works efficiently and bills fairly then you will probably be more likely to consult him.

Finding the Right Attorney

The problem is, how do you find the latter type of attorney. The best way is through a referral from a friend. If someone you know is happy with the service they received from an attorney, you probably will be too. If you cannot locate one through a friend, you can ask people who work at title insurance companies or real estate brokers' offices.

If you do not use a personal referral you can use telephone or newspaper ads or a bar association referral service if one is available in your area. However, this is like playing the lottery and you are as likely to get a bad one as a great one.

One thing to look for when hiring an attorney for a real estate transaction is experience in real estate matters. While all attorneys can legally handle any type of matter, not all are competent to do so. A criminal or divorce lawyer will usually decline a matter out of his or her expertise, but in a slow week he or she may decide it's time to learn about real estate. (The author once reviewed a real estate transaction handled by a criminal lawyer. No deed had ever been prepared and the mortgage was prepared backwards. The attorney explained that he thought that the mortgage also acted as a deed!)

A young attorney just out of law school can offer conscientious service and enthusiasm at a reasonable fee, but the sad truth is that most law schools do not teach students how to handle real estate closings. They concentrate on statutes dating from 1536 and properties that could only be left to male heirs. The only way for new lawyers to learn about real estate transactions is through experience and self-motivated study.

Attorneys Make Mistakes

Our legal system is so complicated that it is sometimes impossible, even for lawyers and judges, to know what the law is. A committee of the Florida Bar and the Florida Board of

Realtors drafted a real estate contract for use in the state and the Florida Supreme Court ruled that part of it was unenforceable. The California Supreme Court was overruled by the United States Supreme Court. If state supreme court judges don't know what the law is how can you expect your lawyer to? The truth is you can't, so the best you can do is deal in good faith and hope you never go to court.

Using this Book and an Attorney

If you want to put together your own deals but are afraid to commit yourself to a large transaction without an attorney, you can use this book to get started, and put together a contract that suits your needs. Then you can have it reviewed by your attorney before you sign it. Rather than paying for 10 or 20 hours of drafting and negotiating, you can hire him or her for an hour or two to review the document with you.

Deal-Killers

Once you have found an attorney who has experience with real estate you should be careful not to let him become a "deal-killer." Real estate agents are well aware of attorneys who prefer to find enough faults with a deal to convince their clients not to go through with it. One reason this may happen is because a dead deal poses no liability for the attorney, but one that closes may cost him plenty if he made a mistake at the closing. And, unlike brokers, attorneys get paid whether the deal closes or not.

To avoid having your deal killed by your attorney you should, first, know as much as possible about the legalities of the deal to begin with, and next, decide exactly what advice you are seeking from him or her.

In most cases you will want an attorney to check the validity of your contract and the correct completion of the closing documents. But in some cases the attorney may interject opinions as to whether the price is too high or too low or whether the deal is a good business decision. Such opinions go beyond legal advice and you should decide ahead of time if this is what you are seeking.

Regular Investors

If you buy and sell property regularly you have more opportunities to run into legal problems. One way to avoid this is to prepare a master contract which you always use. In fact you should have two master contracts, one for buying and one for selling. Since you will be using these regularly, it would be wise to have a real estate attorney review them to be sure there will be no problems with local laws.

If your attorney is uncomfortable with some of the clauses, be sure to find out if they actually present a legal problem or if the discomfort is just because your attorney has never seen them before or is being extra careful. Attorneys are generally conservative and afraid to use new clauses which have not been tried in court. Don't let that stop you from putting together a good contract.

If your attorney says a clause you want to use is invalid or illegal in your jurisdiction you should ask for the specific law or case which says so. Then you should find out if it is still valid or has been overruled. If your attorney says this must be researched, be sure you understand what this will cost. If the cost is prohibitive you should ask if it would be possible to hire a law student to do some research. You can also do some research yourself. There are books on the market which explain how to do legal research. If you cannot find one at a local bookstore or library contact the publisher of this book for more information.

Chapter 3
The Buyer's Position

Usually, the only way to get a good deal on a piece of property is to negotiate. Sellers who offer properties for sale usually do not offer bargains, and those who do usually find buyers immediately. There are a lot of people, including many professionals, keeping an eye on the real estate market. When a property comes on the market at a bargain price, it is usually snapped up quickly.

There are exceptions, of course. Even the multiple listing services occasionally contain bargains. These are properties which have been passed over due to some superficial defect, but which are real bargains. For example many investors never look at listings of one bedroom properties since they are so hard to sell. But a one bedroom house in a great neighborhood with a lot of land might double in price with a small room addition.

Other than these bargains waiting to be plucked, the way to get a good deal on a property is to negotiate. There are many aspects to the sale of a property and while the seller may be firm on some of them, others may be negotiable. The three main areas to negotiate in a real estate deal are:

•**Price.** This is obvious. Usually the price is the most important thing the seller considers. If he gets his price he will feel successful, even if you get concessions on other points which more than compensate you for paying a higher price.

•**Terms.** This is where most of the profit can be made. Even a highly inflated price can be compensated for if the seller will hold the financing at a bargain rate. Even if the seller will not hold the financing, you may be able to convince him to enter into a lease/option agreement, to delay taking part of his proceeds, or to allow assumption of his existing loan.

• **Property.** If the seller needs cash and won't negotiate price or terms, possibly you can get more property included in the deal to make it worthwhile. The owner might include the appliances in the deal, or possibly a vacant lot next door, or even his car or boat. If repairs are needed, the seller may agree to have them done or do them himself. (Be sure the seller is qualified to do the repairs if he wants to do them himself. You don't want him to learn roofing on your dream house!)

Example: The seller demands $100,000 for his property and won't consider a cent less, even though it is worth only $90,000. If the seller will hold the financing at a lower-than-market rate then you may be able to save even more than $10,000 in interest and points.

Example: The seller's price is a little more than you can afford. Try to get the seller to include the appliances, furniture, or even his car in the sale. That will help your budget and let the seller make his sale.

Example: The seller wants a fair price for his property, but you just don't have the down payment. See if the seller will give you a lease/option for a year or two, allowing a credit of part of your rent toward the down payment. Say the fair rent is $500 a month. Offer to pay $600 a month of which $200 is a credit toward the deposit. After two years you will have a credit of $4800.

How Much to Pay

The appraising of real property is taught as if it were a science with formulas and values, but in most cases it is an art. Except in large developments and condominiums where units are nearly identical, each property has its own unique characteristics. Two houses by the same builder may appear identical but they may differ in the direction they face, the trees on the property, the quality of the landscaping, the age of the appliances, the proximity to high-voltage power lines, or any number of factors.

The first criteria which will determine what you should pay for a property should be whether you are buying it for a home or for investment. If you are buying a home you will probably be more concerned with the livability of the house and the neighborhood and the location in relation to your job or schools. If you find a property which ideally suits your needs you will probably be willing to pay a little more for it, especially if you have been looking for a long time.

If you are looking for a property for investment, either for appreciation or cash flow, you will be concerned with the quality of the house and the neighborhood, but even more concerned with the price. Your ultimate profit on a property will in most cases be determined by what you originally paid for it. Many investors realize that most of the profit is made in buying, not selling.

Before making an offer on a property you will need to become familiar with the values of properties in the area you are considering. Do not rely on a real estate agent to advise you if a price is fair or not. There are many excellent agents, but in most cases the law requires the agent to look out for the interests of the seller. In most real estate transactions there is a "seller's" agent who listed the property and a "buyer's" agent who found a buyer. But both agents are usually paid by the seller and are legally obligated to look out for the seller's interest. If you tell "your" agent "I'll pay $100,000 if I have to, but let's offer $90,000" the agent will probably divulge this to the seller.

To learn about values of properties you should plan to spend a lot of time looking at listings, viewing houses and reading the classified ads. Some people spend every weekend, month after month, looking at properties. Unless you work seven days a week at a high paying job, the time is well spent. Familiarity with values will allow you to locate the best property and to know a bargain when you see it.

Buyer's Broker

If you do not have the time to become familiar with properties you can hire what is called a "buyer's broker." This is a real estate agent who works for you rather than the seller. The concept of a buyer's broker is a somewhat new one but it is gaining acceptance rapidly. One reason for the rapid acceptance is the growing number of lawsuits against real estate agents.

Because the buyer's broker represents the buyer and uses his or her efforts to protect the buyer's interests, the buyer's broker is usually paid by the buyer. But when negotiating with a seller, the buyer's broker attempts to adjust the selling price or the amount of seller's broker's commission to compensate the buyer for this additional expense. In some cases the seller's broker will fight this attempt and try to keep the full seller's commission for himself. This often kills the deal.

Fortunately, buyer's brokers are becoming more widely known and used. Once all parties realize that this system protects all of them from liability and does not cost any more in commissions than the existing system everyone will want to do business this way.

Chapter 4
The Seller's Position

For a seller the negotiating starts with the pricing of the property when it is placed on the market. If you get three full-price offers the first day your property is on the market you know it was priced too low.

One way to be sure not to sell too cheap is to start out high and see what offers come in. Many a seller has been shocked to see a property he made a good profit on sell for even more a few months later.

The problem of reaching for the sky is that you may scare off potential buyers. If your property is worth $90,000 and you want to see if you can get $100,000 by listing it at $110,000, you might miss out on all the people who are only looking at properties priced under $100,000.

The first decision you must make is whether you want to sell as soon as possible, or to wait for the best price. If you have been transferred out of town and need to buy a new house you will need a quick sale more than the investor who would like to turn over one of his properties to buy another.

Don't Tie Up Your Property

One goal of your contract should be to close the deal as quickly as possible. The longer the wait the more likely it is that something will go wrong. The buyer might find a better deal, the city might decide to widen the road, or your roof might start to leak.

Time is money and the longer you must wait for payment the more money you lose. Some investors like to set the closing six months or a year away while they earn interest on their money, or look for someone else to sell the property to at a profit (a flip).

Beware of clauses in contracts presented by buyers which give too much time for contingencies. The contract should of course have a set closing date, also called the settlement date, but you should also put time limits on any contingencies. If the buyer wants his contractor to inspect the property, require that this be done in five days. If the sale will be contingent on the buyer getting a loan, require that he obtain a firm commitment within a certain time period and at the going rate. What you don't want to have happen is to get a contract with a distant closing date and have it fall through at the last minute.

Contingent Liability

Another important goal of the contract is to be sure that you do not have any contingent liability once the closing is over. As explained in Chapter 6, state laws may put some liability on you after the closing, but you should not take any more possible liabilities upon yourself in the contract.

If you sign a contract which says that the "seller warrants the air conditioning is in good condition" you could be liable months after the closing if the compressor goes out. It would be much better to say that the air conditioning will be "in working order on the date of closing." If you can schedule the inspection a few days before the closing date that would be better yet so any repairs could be completed and the closing would not have to be delayed.

Selling "As Is"

Stating in the contract that the property is being sold "as is" has long been an iron-clad protection for sellers against claims after the sale. However, it no longer offers complete protection. In several states buyers have successfully sued even when they have bought property "as is."

A clause which specifies which specific items the "as is" clause applies to is usually even stronger than a general "as is" statement, but in one California case the clause "buyer agrees to waive termite clearance and to absolve the seller of any warranty, accepting the house as is" did not protect the seller against a lawsuit for termite infestation and damage!

Even in states where "as is" clauses are respected by the courts they will not protect a seller against major problems which have been intentionally concealed.

Buyers Moving in Early

Occasionally a buyer will want to move into the property, if it is vacant, prior to closing because of an early sale of his house or to avoid motel bills when moving to a new town. In most cases this can work out well, with the buyer paying rent to offset any mortgage expenses the seller may have.

However, some sellers have had bad experiences with buyers who discovered unexpected problems with the property and then attempt to back out of the deal. You will have to decide whether you want to take this risk after meeting the buyers.

In any case the rent should be at least equal to the amount of interest the buyers will be paying once their loan goes through. Also, there should be an adequate deposit against damages.

If the buyers intend to make any alterations or improvements to the property the situation becomes even more complicated. If they tear out a wall and then leave, the cost of the repair could be high. If they put in a pool and back out you should not have to pay them for it or be liable for any liens on the property for the work.

All of these terms should be included in a carefully-worded lease. The rental terms should not be part of the sales contract because it might be construed by a court as an agreement for deed. If this happens you may have to file a foreclosure suit to get them out of your property.

Refund of Deposit

One scam which has been occasionally used on property sellers and real estate agents is to give a personal check as a deposit on a real estate offer and then when the offer is (expectedly) rejected request an immediate refund of the deposit. The refund check is then cashed before the deposit check bounces. When accepting a check as a deposit be sure it is understood that the check must be collected before a refund is made.

Chapter 5
The Art of Negotiating

In some societies negotiation is a way of life and a joy. People get angry if you accept their first offer. They want you to complain and to counteroffer. They love to haggle and to feel they have gotten the best deal they could out of you.

Not so in America. Most Americans hate haggling. Haggling means uncertainty and the possibility of rejection. We never know how high or how low to go and we always worry if we could have gotten a better deal. We would much rather know the bottom line so we can take it or leave it. Recently a car dealer greatly expanded his business by marking its lowest prices on all cars and advertising that the prices were not negotiable.

Since real estate is the most expensive purchase many people make in their lifetimes, putting together a real estate deal is the most important negotiating a person will do. Most real estate is not priced on a take-it-or-leave-it basis, so it is usually necessary to do some negotiating to find out what the best available deal is.

No matter how much you dislike negotiating you should consider that a little discomfort may result in a savings of thousands of dollars. Unless you won the lottery you can probably use the savings for something important in your life. When buying or selling a piece of property you should remember the rule "It can't hurt to ask." By using this as your motto you can considerably benefit.

If you really hate to negotiate you can hire a buyer's broker or an attorney to negotiate for you. While a buyer's broker can often get paid out of funds the seller was expecting to pay as his commission, an attorney will charge you by the hour, usually $100 or more.

If you want to get serious about negotiating there are several good books on the market explaining all the techniques and nuances of negotiation. If a lot of money is involved you might want to get one of these or to hire the services of an attorney or broker to negotiate for you. If not, you can just use the techniques in this chapter to gain a considerable advantage.

Best/Least

To begin you should figure out what is the best deal you can hope for (your best supportable position) and what is the least that you would accept (your worst acceptable position). With these figures you have a range within which to aim. You will know immediately if the deal is worthwhile. Without this you will negotiate aimlessly and may end up with a bad deal.

You should make a list of all the factors which support your best supportable position and use them to argue your case. Use your imagination and come up with as many reasons as possible. When people aim high they often end up high. Asking a lot for something gives the other side the perception, correct or not, that it is worth a lot.

Note, however, that the position must be *supportable*. Don't make a ridiculous offer that no one in their right mind would accept. Otherwise you might not be taken seriously or they might not even bother negotiating with you.

Another danger, if you ask too high and the other side accepts, is that they will be unable to fulfill the deal. If you, as the seller demand too high a price for a property, the buyer may not be able to afford the payments and if you are holding the financing may have to foreclose and go through selling the property again. (Of course, if you got a large deposit you may not mind, but there are other risks to consider such as the buyer filing bankruptcy and tying up the property for a long time, making it unavailable to resell.)

Keep in mind that your worst acceptable position may change. If an offer is made which meets some of your other needs, one part of your position may be worth changing. For example, if you need $100,000 net proceeds from a sale of property to invest for future income you may be able to accept $90,000 or even $80,000 if you hold the mortgage and the buyer pays you higher interest than is otherwise available.

Need, Not Position

One of the biggest mistakes in negotiation is to concentrate on your position and ignore your need. Once people have stated a position it often becomes a matter of pride to maintain that position. In some societies saving face may be important. You must decide if you are more interested in saving face or in making a good deal.

You should analyze the situation, determine your need, and concentrate on that. For example, your position may be that you want to put no more than $10,000 down on the property and that you must refuse a seller's offer which requires $12,000 down. But if the seller will take back a mortgage (which saves you closing costs,) or will include extra appliances in the deal, you may be able to afford the extra $2,000. If you had concentrated on your position of not wanting to put more than $10,000 down you might have lost a good deal.

Sometimes your goals may not be clear even to yourself. A $110,000 house may be cheaper than a $100,000 house if you consider taxes, transportation costs and other variables. Examine your position and decide exactly what is most important to you.

Understand the Other Side

You can negotiate much better if you understand the other side's position and the reasons for it. In other words, as explained in the last paragraph, what is *their* need? If a seller is demanding a large amount of money down, what is his real need? Does he want to pay off a mortgage that you could assume?

Figure out the other side's bottom line and why that is his position or need. Understand their interests and try to formulate your offer to fill their needs as well as yours.

Similarly you should not let the other side know your need. Otherwise they will figure out your worst acceptable position and try to use it to their advantage. You should concentrate on your best supportable position and divert the other side away from factors which reveal your worst acceptable position.

Remember that the other side may feel it is important to save face. Make your offer in such a way as to make them happy to accept it. One way to do this is to make it look like you are making a big change in your position to accommodate them.

Don't Get Emotionally Involved with the Deal

The best negotiators are the ones who don't need the deal. They can walk away from the deal with no regrets and you can feel it. The worst ones are the ones who must have this deal, the ones who are desperate or fell in love with the deal. If you are ready to walk away from the deal if you don't get what you want, and the other side feels it, you will do much better. On the other hand, if you have already decided that you must have this deal you are easy pickings.

If you are also considering other properties or other buyers you will not be pressed to take this one. Even if you don't have others in mind you should act like you do.

Don't Take It Personally

Another mistake in negotiating is to get personally involved with your opponents. Once you have met them a few times, perhaps found out you are from the same home town, become cordial, you may feel awkward in not accepting whatever they offer. It is not easy to turn someone down, especially someone with whom you have just made friends.

Some people are soft negotiators and others hard. Some give in easily just to avoid disagreement and others hold out until they get everything they want. If you are the former you will easily be taken advantage of by the latter.

One way to avoid such a situation is to negotiate through an agent. It is easy for an agent to become best friends with the other side and to praise their position, but to explain that he has no control over your decision. One advantage of using a land trust, for instance, is that a buyer can be friendly with the seller and still easily explain that the trust has certain rules which must be followed. But that is another book...

Another variation is to use the "good guy/bad guy" approach. One party can do the negotiating and then blame their spouse or partner for not agreeing to the deal. The bad guy never meets personally with the other side, he just vetoes deals from the background.

Don't lock into a position or each change will be difficult. Keep in mind the worst acceptable result which you have already established and don't worry about the intermediate steps. Be open to all possible options and to any new suggestions the other side may have. There may be an alternative that you have not even considered.

Keep in mind that the other side may be taking his or her side personally. Don't criticize the other side personally or say anything that makes the other side more attached to his or her position.

Start at Your Best Supportable Position

Starting at your best supportable position may sound obvious, but some people give away their worst acceptable position right away. Keep in mind that it can't hurt to ask and try your best supportable position. Many people have started with ridiculously high figures and been surprised to have them accepted.

You only get one chance to state your opening position and you usually can't go higher. Suppose you list your vacant lot for sale at $20,000 and the day the listing is published you get five offers at full price. Obviously you started too low. And it may be too late to ask for more.

Turn the Tables

Whether you are the buyer or seller, when you enter negotiations on a property the other side will probably be expecting to be doing the screening. The seller wants to screen for the best price and the buyer wants to screen for the best property.

If you begin the negotiation by listing your needs and asking if the other side can meet them then you have turned the tables. The other side will then be put in the position of wondering if they can meet *your* needs. Meeting your needs will then be the primary goal and their needs may be forgotten.

For example, the owner of an unusual expensive property did not know if anyone would want such a property. So the ad for the property merely listed its best features without a photo or address and stated that the buyer must have at least $100,000 cash and a net worth of at least a million dollars. Dozens of people called to see if they could qualify for this exclusive offer and it sold at full asking price!

Your Last Shot

Once you think you may be able to make a deal, why not ask for one last concession? You like the property, the price is acceptable and the sellers has agreed to your terms. Try something like, "If you throw in the washer and dryer I'll take it." As we keep saying, it can't hurt to ask.

Chapter 6
Federal and Local Laws

The laws governing real estate have changed more in the last few years than they have in the last few centuries. Ancient legal doctrines such as *caveat emptor* (buyer beware) and "sanctity of contract" have been abandoned in favor of policies which allow courts to protect people from themselves and find someone with money to pay for each injury.

While the purpose of this book is to help you draft the best contract for your interest, it must be understood that there are laws which may overrule your contract. More about how an excessively strong contract can work against you is contained in the next chapter. This chapter discusses laws which may affect your contract rights.

Some examples of new developments in the law which affect the sale of real estate are:

• In Vermont a seller of property was found guilty of manslaughter when the buyers of his house died from carbon monoxide poisoning caused by a defective driveway defroster.

• In New York a seller of property was forced to take it back when the buyer convinced an appeals court that the house was haunted.

• In Florida the sellers of a house were liable for expensive repairs because they did not disclose a leak in the roof.

The basic laws controlling the purchase and sale of real estate are ancient laws which originated in England hundreds of years ago. However, because each state has its own statutes and court cases, the legal rights of buyers and sellers and the validity of certain clauses may vary from state to state. Also, our federal government has passed numerous laws in recent years which control real estate sales.

The following are some of the most important laws which affect the sale of real estate. Keep in mind, though, that new laws are being passed every day somewhere in this country and you should find out if any of them affect what you want to do.

Federal Laws

FHA/VA Loans. If a purchase will be financed by a loan guaranteed by the Federal Housing Authority or the Department of Veterans Affairs (formerly known as the Veterans Administration) then certain language must be included in the contract. An FHA/VA clause is included in this book.

Discrimination. Since the Civil Rights Act of 1964 it has been illegal to discriminate in the sale of real estate based upon race, sex religion or nationality (Title 42 United States Code, sections 3601-17). Even policies which do not clearly discriminate, but have the effect of discriminating are illegal under this law. The following are the basic rules under the law:

• <u>Remedy.</u> A victim of discrimination under this section can file a civil suit, a HUD complaint or request the U.S. Attorney General to prosecute. Damages can include actual losses and punitive damages of up to $1000.

• <u>Limitation.</u> The complaint must be brought within 180 days.

• <u>Exemptions.</u> This law does not apply to single family homes if the owner owns 3 or fewer, if there is no more than one sale within 24 months, if the person does not own any interest in more than 3 at one time, and if no real estate agent or discriminatory advertisement is used. It also does not apply to a property which is owner-occupied if it has 4 or fewer units.

• <u>Coercion or Intimidation.</u> Where coercion or intimidation is used to cause discrimination there is no limit to when the action can be brought or to the amount of damages.

The Civil Rights Act §1982 (42 USC 1982) is a law similar to the above statute but where the above applies to any policy which has a discriminatory effect, this law applies only where it can be proved that the person had an *intent* to discriminate.

• <u>Remedy.</u> Actual damages plus *unlimited* punitive damages.

• <u>Limitation.</u> None.

• <u>Exemptions.</u> None.

Environmental Hazards. To avoid having taxpayers pay for the cleanup of the environment, Congress has passed the Comprehensive Environmental Response, Compensation, and Liability Act (CERCLA or Superfund) 42 U.S.C. §§9601-9657 (1982). This law puts the cleanup burden on property owners even if they are innocent of causing any pollution.

For example, if you buy a piece of property and later find out it is contaminated with pollutants, you may be personally liable for the cleanup. If the property only cost you $50,000 and the cleanup cost is $500,000, you can still be forced to pay for the cleanup out of your other assets. There is no way you can wipe out this liability, even through bankruptcy.

Putting the property in a trust or corporation will not protect you, and even if you sell the property you may be held liable many years later just for having owned the property once in the past.

Because of this it is important to avoid buying property unless you are sure it is free of contamination. In a residential subdivision there is less of a risk than on a busy highway where a toxic factory might have existed in the past. However, if toxic waste travels underground to a residential property the owner is still liable for cleanup.

The risk of serious pollution on most properties is small so there is no point in avoiding buying real estate altogether for this slight risk. Rather you should shop wisely. You can protect against liability by finding out who the former owners were and by having an environmental audit done on the property but this is expensive and may make the property not be worth buying.

Foreign Buyers

Federal tax law requires buyers of real property to withhold taxes from the proceeds of purchases from foreign persons or companies. If this is not done then the buyer may be liable for paying the tax personally.

To avoid the liability the seller should obtain a "non-foreign person" affidavit from the seller. If the seller is a foreign person and cannot provide such an affidavit, then the buyer should consult an attorney or tax specialist.

RESPA

The Real Estate Settlement Procedures Act (12 USC §2601 et seq.) contains federal rules which apply to many residential closings. One requirement is that the closing statement be done on the form approved by the Department of Housing and Urban Development (HUD-1). This law will be of concern to the attorney or title agent who handles the closing of your transaction.

Interstate Land Sales

To attempt to eliminate fraud in interstate sales of land, Congress passed the Interstate Land Sales Full Disclosure Act (15 USC §1701 et seq.) This law requires full disclosure of certain information by those who are selling vacant land.

Tax Laws

An explanation of all of the tax ramifications of a real estate transaction is beyond the scope of this book, but anyone buying or selling real estate should be aware of the following possible tax aspects of the deal:

• **Installment sales rules.** In some cases a seller can be taxed in the year of sale for income which has not been received.

• **Residence replacement rule.** The gain on the sale of a residence can be deferred if a residence of equal or greater value is purchased within twenty-four months before or after the sale.

• **Over 55 rule.** A person over 55 can avoid paying taxes on up to $125,000 profit on the sale of a primary residence.

• **Tax-free exchanges.** Under section 1031 of the Internal Revenue Code you may trade one piece of property for like-kind property without paying any tax on the transaction.

• **Passive income.** Under the Tax Reform Act of 1986 losses of over $25,000 from a real estate investment may only be deducted against other passive income.

• **Depreciation.** You may depreciate the value of the building (but not the land) on investment property over a set number of years, from your taxable income.

• **Personal property.** Personal property can be depreciated faster than the building. If personal property is included with an investment property, you may want to assign more of the purchase price to those items.

If you feel that any of these rules may apply to you, you should research the matter further before signing a contract. For example, for the "over 55" rule to apply you must have lived in the property for three of the previous five years. What a shame it would be if you had only lived there two and one-half years and signed a contract forcing you to close within three months! For exchanges to qualify as tax-free, the properties must qualify as "like-kind" under strict IRS rules.

There are more specialized rules concerning low-income housing, interest deduction limitations, construction interest deduction, historic renovations and tax exempt bonds. Check with a knowledgeable tax advisor or consult a tax guide for more information.

Local Laws

Some states, such as Utah, Texas and Wisconsin, require certain forms to be used for real estate transactions. Other states require certain clauses to be included in such contracts. And some local governments such as cities and counties have their own rules. These laws may change at any time and it would be impossible for a book of this type to be up to date for every locality.

Therefore it is important for you to verify that your contract complies with your local laws. One way to do this is to consult an attorney who specializes in real estate law or an active real estate broker. Another way is to obtain copies of real estate contracts used in your area from brokers and office supply stores. Be sure to ask if there are any addendum forms available.

Laws which you might not ever conceive of do exist, so be sure to do a thorough check of what laws might apply. The following are some laws which exist in some areas.

Environmental Laws

Some states, such as Connecticut, Florida, Indiana, Massachusetts, Montana, New Hampshire, New Jersey and Virginia have laws requiring sellers to disclose information about environmental hazards. Such hazards would include asbestos, lead, radon, urea-formaldehyde insulation and underground storage tanks. Most states do not require sellers to have their properties tested for these hazards, but they must disclose any hazards of which they are aware.

For this reason it may be unwise to test your house for lead paint, asbestos, or other materials, because if they are found and you fail to disclose the fact you risk charges of concealment and misrepresentation. If you do not do any testing you will have nothing to disclose.

While such disclosures may scare away some potential buyers and make it harder to sell the property, in they long run they may prove to be a protection for sellers. Like the warnings on cigarette packages, they may protect sellers from costly lawsuits if the buyer is injured sometime in the future.

It can be expected that these laws will get stricter and that before long all properties may have to be inspected before they are sold. For this reason it is a good idea to check out a property when buying it so that you are not stuck with paying for a big problem when you decide to sell.

Note: Some states require certain language in the radon clause or other notice. Be sure to check if your state has such a requirement.

Known Defects

In over thirty states there are voluntary disclosure forms used for informing buyers of known defects in a property. Each year similar bills are filed in several states and soon all states may have them. In some states, such as Delaware and Tennessee, the proposed disclosure applies to commercial properties as well as residential. In California the form is mandatory and in Maine it is mandatory only if a real estate broker is used in the sale. In many states real estate brokers require disclosure forms from sellers to protect themselves from liability.

As with environmental hazards disclosures, these forms can protect the seller from future lawsuits. Remember that you need only disclose *known* defects. If a neighbor or former owner told you about some possible problem on the property but you have never experienced the problem yourself you don't actually *know* of it.

Of course if you take apart a wall and find termite damage you shouldn't patch it up and pretend you never saw it. If the buyer can prove the patch was fresh you can be liable for misrepresentation. In some states, if something on the property is found to be inherently dangerous then the seller can be held liable for any injuries caused by it.

If you don't know about some aspect of the property, admit it. A disclosure that you don't know if the roof leaks would be better than claiming it definitely didn't leak, especially if you never actually looked in the attic.

Implied Warranties

In some states the courts have held that builders can be held liable for defects in properties they have sold. Rather than make the "buyer beware," the courts have noted that builders are more knowledgeable about their profession and should not be able to sell defective products without liability.

Stigmatized Properties

Some people become upset with the fact that a tragedy such as a murder or a suicide took place in a house. Often this is the first thing the buyers learn from neighbors so it can quickly result in a lawsuit for recision.

At least twenty states say that such facts do not have to be disclosed. As mentioned previously, a New York appeals court allowed recision when a buyer convinced the court that her house was haunted. In California the seller does not have to disclose a death if it occurred more than three years before the sale.

It will be interesting to see how the courts rule in cases where the last occupant had AIDS. While some people will argue that it is important to disclose this, others will argue that such matters are private and must not be disclosed.

Real Estate Licensees

In some states persons who are licensed as real estate brokers or sales agents must disclose this fact on any contracts they execute for themselves. The rationale is that they have special knowledge about properties and they might be using it to take advantage of a person who is less sophisticated.

Speculation Tax

In the District of Columbia (but not in Russia) there is a special tax on persons who buy a property and then sell it at a profit. Perhaps it's considered a sin tax.

Zoning and Land Use Laws

Today nearly all land is subject to zoning or land use laws. These laws can make it impossible to use a property for some activities. Everyone knows that businesses are not allowed in some residential areas, but some laws also forbid the parking of boats or RVs in the yard or cars on the street. Some purchasers have been badly disappointed to discover that they had to find other storage facilities for their vehicles after the closing on their new house.

As explained in the discussion in this book on zoning clauses, you should make any purchase of property contingent on the zoning not interfering with your needs.

Chapter 7
Overreaching

If a judge feels a contract is too one-sided or that a weak party was taken advantage of by a strong party, the judge can, in some cases, change the terms of the contract. The doctrine of sanctity of contract has given way, in our modern world, to a view that the weak must be protected from the strong, and even from themselves.

Therefore, an exceedingly strong contract may not work in your favor in every case. If your "iron clad" contract is ever taken to court a judge may be so shocked by it that he or she would rule against you no matter what your contract says.

As mentioned earlier, one tactic used by some purchasers is to prepare a contract that is totally one-sided and have it printed up with the words "approved form" at the top. Since most people, and even some attorneys, only read the material typed on a contract, contracts with ridiculous terms in the fine print are often signed.

If such a case went to court and it was determined that an unsophisticated seller was clearly taken advantage of, a judge could easily find a reason to declare the contract void. The incident might also result in a newspaper article or a fraud investigation. This is especially likely if the person using the strong contract had a real estate license.

That is not to say that a strong contract should *never* be used. Most disputes never get to court and if the other party backs out of the deal you can sometimes just walk away and not have your contract tested in court.

Some people put little boxes for initials next to each clause which might be considered controversial. This might help in convincing a judge that the other person was aware of the clause, but it would not keep a contract from being declared void if it were considered unconscionable by the judge.

Traditionally, the best way to protect a deal from being declared void is to include a severability clause. This is a clause which says that if one part of the contract is declared void the rest of the contract will not be affected.

However, in an overly strong real estate contract this kind of clause may backfire. For example, suppose you are buying a $40,000 property and offer $50,000 for it if the owner will take an unsecured note at 2% interest. If the case went to court and a judge thought that an unsecured note at 2% was unconscionable, you would not want the deal to go through at $50,000.

A problem of this kind would most likely come up where one party was unsophisticated and did not understand the contract and later thinks he or she was cheated. When sophisticated investors make such deals with elderly blind widows the courts, newspapers and consumer fraud departments have a field day.

The chance of having problems like this can be lessened by having someone more knowledgeable assist the person you are dealing with. Some investors even insist that the other party get a lawyer or that they sign a paper stating that they know they should have one but have decided against it. Of course, if the offer is really outrageous the attorney or other advisor might convince the person not to sign it.

Chapter 8
Basic Clauses

The minimum that a real estate contract must contain to be legally enforceable is:

1. Identification of the parties
2. Description of the property
3. Clear terms of payment
4. Some "consideration" such as a deposit
5. An offer and an acceptance

However, it is important to both the buyer and the seller to have other terms and contingencies. A buyer would probably want the sale contingent upon receiving a clear title insurance policy and termite clearance. A seller would want an earnest money deposit to bind the deal and to be sure to receive certified funds.

A real estate contract should spell out the terms of the transaction in as much detail as possible. Some buyers and real estate agents present offers which are very vague and then fight over the details at closing. The idea is, the less said the less there is to disagree with, we can haggle at the closing. These are the deals which most often fall through. If all of the terms are spelled out in the contract then neither party can back out of the deal.

On the following pages different versions are given for each possible clause. Depending on whether you are buying or selling, you can choose the version which is in your best interest.

Most people do not even question many of the terms in a printed form. They read just what's typed in the blanks. If a form contract says that the seller pays for the termite report they wouldn't question it. If the form says the buyer pays and you cross it out and type in "Seller," they will scream! For this reason you might want to have your contract typeset as explained in Chapter 1.

At the end of this book there are five contract forms. One of these should be suitable for any normal situation. To make amendments to the basic form an "Addendum" is provided. Additional clauses from this book can be added to the basic contract forms by using this addendum.

PARTIES & AGREEMENT

Explanation:

Two of the most basic parts of the contract are the parties and the statement that they agree to a sale and purchase. The form of the clause is not important, but what is filled in the clause is very important. Don't forget to get the phone number. You might need to contact the other side if a problem arises.

Buyer's View:

The buyer will want to be sure that he gets the signatures of all of the owners of the property. If several people own the property and only some of them sign, then it will be impossible to force the other owner to go through with the contract. (However, it might be possible to sue the ones who signed if they represented that they had the authority to sell.)

Buyers should decide when making the contract how they wish to take title. If they take as "tenants in common" then when one dies his or her share goes to whoever inherits their estate. If they take title as "joint tenants with full right of survivorship" then when one dies his or her share goes to the other owner. In some states a married couple may take as "tenants by the entireties" which offers some protections, for example, from creditors.

Seller's View:

In most cases the seller would prefer to have the contract signed by someone with substantial assets or good credit. If the seller will be holding the financing, this will be especially important. If the buyer will be paying all cash it would not matter who signed, but if the buyer has no assets and ties the property up for months, the seller will have no recourse.

Sellers should be careful of offers from corporations or trustees. These can be "shell" entities with no assets and can cost the seller a great deal of money. For example, if a property were sold to a shell corporation with little money down the corporation could collect rents or strip the property while the seller goes through months of court proceedings to get the property back

PARTIES:_____ as "Buyer" of
_____ Phone:_____and
_____ as "Seller" of
_____ Phone:_____hereby
agree that the Buyer shall buy and the Seller shall sell real property described below under the following terms and conditions:

PURCHASE PRICE

Clause #1:

The full purchase price shall be $_____ payable as follows:

a) Deposit held in escrow by _____ $_____

b) New mortgage* to be obtained by Buyer _____
_____ $_____

c) Subject to [ ] , or assumption of [ ] mortgage* to _____
_____ with interest rate of _____%, payable $_____
per month, having an approximate balance of....................... $_____

d) Mortgage* and Note to be held by seller at ___% interest payable
_____ for _____ years in the amount of.... $_____

e) Other _____
_____ $_____

f) Balance to close (U.S. cash, certified or cashier's check)
subject to adjustments and prorations, plus closing costs.... $_____

Total .... $_____

*In some areas the words "Deed of Trust" are used instead of "Mortgage."

Notes:

a) The seller would prefer a larger deposit of at least 10% of the sales price, held by himself or his attorney. This way the buyer will not be tempted to walk away from the deal. The buyer would prefer a small deposit, such as $100 or $500, held by a neutral party such as a title company or the real estate broker.

b) The buyer would want to specify the terms of the mortgage he wants to get. Otherwise if rates go up he will be required to buy the property at whatever the going rate is. See the clause for "Financing Contingency."

c) If the buyer **assumes** the mortgage he agrees to be legally bound to pay it. If the buyer takes the property **subject to** the mortgage, he has no legal obligation to pay it (though he could lose the property if he does not). The seller prefers that the buyer assume the mortgage and should use another clause which requires that the seller be released from further liability on the loan. Otherwise the seller could be sued years later if the buyer fails to pay the loan. The buyer prefers to buy the property subject to the mortgage with no assumption of the liability. The buyer wants the mortgage terms filled in so that if they are not what as described he can rescind the contract.

d) This clause should clearly spell out the payment terms. The other terms of the mortgage that the seller will hold should be set out in another clause in the contract.

e) Use this space if there is a second mortgage, a property to be used as part of a trade, or any other form of payment. If a small deposit was made, then the seller should require additional deposit money after any contingencies in the contract have been eliminated.

f) This is the amount that the buyer will need to have at closing in addition to the initial deposit.

If you are customizing a contract and know that you will not need all of the options in the previous clause you can use a shorter version to suit your needs:

Clause #2:   The purchase price shall be $_____.

Clause #3:   The purchase price shall be $_____ subject to the following terms and conditions:_____

_____

_____.

Clause #4:   The purchase price shall be determined by a _____ appraisal done by an appraiser acceptable to the Buyer and Seller.

Note: The type of appraisal in Alternate clause #3 might be FHA (Federal Housing Administration), VA (Veterans' Administration which was changed to the Department of Veteran Affairs), MAI (Member, Appraisal Institute), or some other entity which provides appraisals.

CONVEYANCE

Seller's View: The seller would like to get his money without further obligation and the best way to do this is to sign a quit claim or fee simple deed. But in most cases a seller will need to sign a warranty deed. If the seller is selling property which he bought and for which he received a warranty deed, giving a warranty deed is no problem. However, if the seller inherited the property or received part of it by quit claim deed or court settlement then the seller would be better off conveying by quit claim deed or fee simple deed.

Definitions: A **quit claim deed** is a deed which says, in effect, "I don't know what I own, but whatever it is I convey it to you." In some states a quit claim deed is a warning to a buyer that the seller doesn't think he owns the property, but in most states such a deed does not create any negative assumption. A **fee simple deed** is one that merely conveys all rights to a piece of property. In most areas a **general warranty deed** is one in which a seller guarantees that he has good title to the property and a **special warranty deed** is a deed in which the seller doesn't guarantee that he has good title, but does guarantee that he hasn't done anything which would affect the title. However, in some states these definitions are reversed.

Clause #1:   Conveyance shall be by fee simple deed.

Clause #2:   Conveyance shall be by Special Warranty Deed subject to matters excepted in this Contract.

Clause #3:   Conveyance shall be by General Warranty Deed subject to matters excepted in this Contract.

Buyer's View: The buyer would prefer a warranty deed guarantying that the title is good so that if there are problems with the title he can get his money back from the seller. However, if, as is usual in most states, the buyer will receive title insurance, then the type of deed is not as important to the buyer as it is to the title company. The buyer would also like a bill of sale on the personal property to prove that he has bought it. Without a bill of sale, a neighbor could come over and say that the lawn mower in the garage belongs to him and was merely borrowed by the seller.

Clause: Conveyance shall be by General Warranty Deed subject only to matters excepted in this Contract. Personal property shall be conveyed by an absolute Bill of Sale with warranty of title subject only to such liens as provided herein.

PROPERTY DESCRIPTION

Seller's View:

The seller does not want to promise to sell more than he owns. Many a seller has been sued when the property he owned turned out to be less than he described in the sales contract. Where a lot in a subdivision is being sold, the legal description usually consists of the lot number and plat. But where rural or unplatted land is being sold the boundary can be affected by a neighbor's fence, the movement of a stream or many other factors.

The best description would be the exact description of the property from a previous deed, unless part of the property has since been sold or taken for road widening. In many cases the seller could use the street address, but this might cause problems. If the seller also owned the vacant lot next door the buyer might assume that it was part of the property. Adding the *approximate* lot size or acreage would make the description more accurate and the contract more enforceable. If the deed of purchase is available it would usually be safe and even more accurate to use the description contained on it.

Definitions:

Have you noticed real estate signs which offer a piece of property described as "6.5 acres MOL"? **MOL** means More or Less and this is always added to the description so that the buyer cannot sue if the land turns out to be 6.4 acres after it is surveyed.

Buyer's View:

The buyer's position is the opposite of the seller. He wants to know exactly what he is buying. Some properties have been found to be a fraction of what the seller described them as. When this is discovered after the closing an expensive lawsuit usually results. Unless the property is part of a platted subdivision the buyer would be well advised to obtain a survey of the property. For extra caution the buyer could make the contract contingent upon the survey being satisfactory. Of course the buyer would prefer that the seller pay the cost of the survey (See the Survey Clause.) When the buyer is relying on a description provided by a real estate agent, he may want to state something like, "...as described in MLS Listing Number 123456."

Clause:

Street Address _____

Legal Description:_____

_____

_____

_____

OTHER AGREEMENTS

Both Parties' View: Neither party wants the other to say that they were promised something not in the contract, or that the contract did not cover everything that they had agreed upon. While it is often difficult to prove the terms of an oral agreement it is better to make it clear that there was no intent to rely on anything not put into the contract.

Buyer's View: If the buyer is relying on some other document such as a listing of the property or a survey or sketch provided by the seller, then that document should be mentioned in the contract and made a part of the contract. For example, see the explanation on the previous page.

Clause: No prior or present agreements or representations shall be binding upon the parties unless incorporated into this Contract. No modification or change in this Contract shall be valid or binding unless in writing and signed by the party to be bound thereby.

F.H.A./V.A.

Explanation: In the event the purchase will be financed by an F.H.A. or V.A. loan, one of the following clauses is necessary. These are clauses required by the government regulations. They should not be changed. Since the Veterans Administration was changed to the Department of Veteran Affairs, the initials may change in the V.A. clause.

F.H.A. Clause: It is expressly agreed that, notwithstanding any other provisions of this contract, the Purchaser shall not be obligated to complete the purchase of the property described herein or to incur any penalty by forfeiture of earnest money deposits or otherwise unless the Seller has delivered to the Purchaser a written statement issued by the Federal Housing Commissioner setting forth the appraised value of the property (excluding closing costs) for the mortgage insurance purpose of not less than $_____ which statement the Seller agrees to deliver to the Purchaser promptly after such appraised value is made available to Seller.

The Purchaser shall, however, have the privilege and option of proceeding with the consummation of this contract without regard to the amount of the appraised valuation made by the Federal Housing Commissioner. The appraised valuation is arrived at to determine the maximum mortgage the Department of Housing and Urban Development will insure. HUD does not warrant the value or the condition of the property. The Purchaser should satisfy himself/herself that the price and condition of the property are acceptable.

V.A. Clause: It is expressly agreed that, notwithstanding any other provision of this contract, the Purchaser shall not incur any penalty by forfeiture of earnest money or otherwise be obligated to complete the purchase of the property described herein, if the contract purchase price or cost exceeds the reasonable value of the property established by the Veterans Administration. The Purchaser shall, however, have the privilege and option of proceeding with the consummation of this contract without regard to the amount of the reasonable value established by the Veterans Administration. Purchaser agrees that should Purchaser elect to complete the purchase at an amount in excess of the reasonable value established by V.A., Purchaser shall pay such excess amount in cash from a source which Purchaser agrees to disclose to the V.A. and which Purchaser represents will not be borrowed funds except as approved by V.A.

INSULATION CLAUSE

Explanation:

Effective September 29, 1980, sellers of **new** homes, condominiums and cooperatives to consumers are required by federal law (16 C.F.R. 460) to provide detailed information about the insulation. If the information is not available when the contract is signed the seller must agree to provide it as soon as it is available.

Clause:

INSULATION. The insulation in the property is as follows:

1. Exterior walls are insulated with _____ to a thickness of ___ inches which according to manufacturer will yield an R-value of R-____.

2. Interior walls are insulated with _____ to a thickness of ___ inches which according to manufacturer will yield an R-value of R-____.

3. Ceilings of air-conditioned areas are insulated with _____ to a thickness of ___ inches which according to manufacturer will yield an R-value of R-____.

4. Garage ceilings, if any, are insulated with _____ _____ to a thickness of ___ inches which according to manufacturer will yield an R-value of R-____.

5. Garage partition walls of air-conditioned areas are insulated with _____ to a thickness of ___ inches which according to manufacturer will yield an R-value of R-____.

Chapter 9
Recommended Clauses

It takes many clauses to comprise a good real estate contract. Many issues must be dealt with and many potential problems avoided. It is in ironing out the details of a deal that conflicts usually come up. On way to approach a deal is to agree to the basics and fight over the details later, perhaps at closing. The better way is to agree on all the details in the contract negotiation and then go to a closing that is short and sweet.

The clauses in this chapter will help you go to a smooth closing. You might have to fight over each clause while putting the contract together. You might have to give in on some. But if you work out all of the little details in the contract there will be no surprises at the last minute and there will be less chance the deal will fall through. Many sales have failed to close when the parties discovered that they really didn't agree on everything and that they were unable to resolve their differences.

The clauses in this chapter should allow you to clearly put into writing every aspect of your real estate purchase. If you are doing something especially complicated you might want to check at a law library for a some of the books written for lawyers on real estate contracts, or you can take a seminar on creative real estate contracts. But for most people this should cover all of their needs.

ACCEPTANCE

Buyer's View: The buyer wants the seller to have to quickly decide whether or not he will accept the offer, but wants to have as long as possible to decide himself if he is given a counter-offer.

Clause: [If offer is made to seller] Seller shall have until _____ _____, 19___ at ___ o'clock __m to accept this Contract.

Comments: With this clause a seller must decide within the time specified or the offer is void, but if the seller presents a counter-offer, it remains open until the seller withdraws it.

Neutral Clause: If this offer is not executed by both parties on or before _____, 19___, it shall be void and Buyer's deposit returned.

Seller's View: The seller wants time to shop for offers but wants the buyer to decide quickly.

Clause: [If offer is made to buyer] Buyer shall have until _____ _____, 19___ at _____ o'clock __m to accept this Contract.

AGREEMENT FOR DEED

Explanation:

In some cases the parties may want to use an "Agreement for Deed," an "Installment land contract, or a "Contract for Deed" rather than an actual deed of the property. Some states have laws which make using these contracts risky for the buyer who could lose the property even after years of making payments. But in other states they are used successfully by both buyers and sellers.

The most common use of such agreements is where the buyer has little money to put down and the seller is willing to help with some of the financing but wants to be sure that the first mortgage is paid on time each month. In some states, where these agreements must be foreclosed like mortgages, it is risky to sell a property to a buyer who has put little or no money down because the buyer can stay in the property for months without making a payment.

In a conventional sale the seller deeds the property over to the buyer and the buyer then gives a mortgage or deed of trust to a bank or other lender. In an agreement for deed the buyer does not yet get the deed. The agreement states that at a later date he will receive the deed if he complies with all the terms. Such agreements are often used when a buyer has little money to put down. Sometimes they provide that the buyer will be given a deed and be allowed to assume the first mortgage after he builds up a certain amount of equity.

In another clause (Purchase Price) the contract must also spell out what the interest rate and payment terms are.

Buyer's View:

The buyer wants a long grace period, wants the agreement to be assumable, and does not want a prepayment penalty.

Clause:

In the event the property will be sold by Agreement (Contract) for Deed, said agreement shall contain no prepayment penalty, be fully assumable and allow a 30-day grace period on late payments. Purchaser shall have a first right of refusal at any time Seller desires to sell his interest in the Agreement.

Seller's View:

The seller does not want a long grace period and does not want the agreement to be assumed without his approval.

Clause:

In the event property will be sold by Agreement (Contract) for Deed said agreement shall contain a 10-day grace period and provide that if any interest in the property is transferred (other than a subordinate lien or lease without an option) the remaining balance shall become immediately due and payable.

ALLOCATION OF PURCHASE PRICE

Buyer's View: If the property is being purchased for investment the buyer usually would like as much of the purchase price as possible allocated to personal property which can be depreciated quickly. When buying a residence the buyer would usually not want any amount allocated to personal property because he wants a higher basis in the real estate.

Seller's View: If the property is his residence the seller would prefer to allocate as much as possible of the purchase price to personal property because that would lower his taxable profit on the real estate. (Selling used household goods at less than their purchase price would not be taxable.) The seller's position on investment property would depend on his tax situation and this should be discussed with a tax advisor.

Clause: The parties agree that the allocation of the purchase price is $_____ for the land, $_____ for the buildings and $_____ for the personal property. The parties agree that this sale is indivisible even though the amounts have been allocated separately.

Clause: [Add to the end of the "Personal Property" clause" on page 67.] The portion of the purchase price allocated to the personal property is $_____.

Note: If it appears that the parties have agreed to ridiculous allocation amounts solely to avoid taxes the IRS may ignore it and substitute what it feels is a more reasonable allocation. The second sentence is included so that one party does not try to buy only part of the property based upon a favorable allocation.

APPROVAL

Buyer's View: The buyer may want to have the contract contingent upon the approval of his partner, spouse, attorney, or other advisor. Where a partner is involved it is usually necessary to obtain their approval to complete the deal. But in other cases, the approval of a third party can be used to give the buyer the right to get out of the deal. In this way a buyer can lock in a deal and then after thinking about it for a few weeks say that his wife didn't approve. The danger with using such a clause is that if the seller wanted to get out of the deal and took it to court, the court could rule that the contract was not binding upon the buyer so that it would also not be binding on the seller. The buyer usually would like the contingency to apply right up until the closing in case he needs to back out of the deal.

Clause #1:   This Contract is contingent upon the approval of Buyer's spouse.

Clause #2:   This Contract is contingent upon the approval of Buyer's partner.

Clause #3:   This Contract is contingent upon the approval of Buyer's attorney.

Seller's View: The seller does not want any contingencies in the contract, but if there are any he wants them to last for only a few days so that he can then put his property back on the market. In some cases the seller might want to sign the contract but make it subject to his attorney's approval.

Clause #1:   [PREFER NO CLAUSE]

Clause #2:   This Contract is contingent upon the approval of Buyer's spouse within _____ hours.

Clause #3:   This Contract will be in full force and effect unless _____ objects in writing on or before _____[date]_____, at __[time]__.

Comment: It is usually good to have an attorney review a contract before accepting (or presenting) it to be sure that there is nothing in it which would be legally objectionable, or misleading. However, a problem sometimes comes up when the attorney leaves the realm of legal advice and starts giving business advice. For example, attorneys have been known to tell their client that a price was too low (or too high) or that the property is not a good investment. Some people may be glad to have such advice. For others it may sour what was thought of as a good deal. When using an attorney be sure you know what type of advice you are seeking. See Chapter 2.

ASSIGNMENT

Buyer's View: Buyer would like the right to assign the contract to another purchaser or to a corporation or trust. If the seller will be holding the financing the buyer could avoid personal liability by assigning the contract to a corporation.

Clause #1:   Buyer may assign this Contract and all rights and obligations hereunder to another person, corporation or trustee.

Clause #2:   This Contract is fully assignable.

Clause #3:   This Contract is fully assignable. Buyer shall have the right to show the property to prospective purchasers prior to closing.

Comments: Clause #1 makes it clearer that the contract can be assigned to a corporation or trustee which would have no personal liability. If Clause #2 is used a seller could at least make the argument that he relied on the buyer's personal worth and might try to back out of the contract if the buyer assigned the contract to a shell corporation or trustee. Clause #3 makes it clear that the buyer intends to resell the property (presumably at a profit) prior to the time he takes title.

Seller's View: A seller who is receiving all cash out of the sale probably wouldn't care who is buying it so assignability wouldn't be a problem, but where a seller will hold a mortgage or where he will remain liable on the mortgage, he should have someone with substantial assets personally signing the note.

Clause #1:   This Contract is personal to the parties and is not assignable.

Clause #2:   Buyer may not assign this Contract without the approval by Seller of any assignee's credit worthiness.

Comments: If the buyer is to make a substantial down payment and the seller would be glad to get the property back without a deficiency judgment, assignability would not be a problem.

Note: In some jurisdictions a contract **is assignable** unless it states otherwise; in other jurisdictions it **is not assignable** unless it states otherwise. If the law in your jurisdiction is well-settled you could rely on that and leave the clause out. However, there is less chance of a lawsuit if you put it clearly in the contract.

ATTORNEY'S FEES

Usual View:
If the loser will have to pay both parties' attorneys' fees in a law suit then neither party will be as eager to file a law suit unless they have a very good case. Stipulating that the loser will pay both sides attorneys' fees makes litigation less likely in a close case.

Another View:
If one party has a lawyer in the family or on retainer, he may want to sue even if his case is weak, because he doesn't have to worry about paying the other side's attorney's fees.

A Third View:
Because of the high cost of attorney's fees, some people prefer to put an arbitration clause in all of their contracts. Arbitration is usually a lot less expensive than going to court.

Clause #1:
In connection with any litigation, including appellate proceedings, arising out of this Contract, the prevailing party shall be entitled to recover reasonable attorneys' fees and costs.

Clause #2:
In the event of any litigation arising out of this Contract each party shall be responsible for his or her own attorneys' fees and costs.

Clause #3:
In the event [Buyer or Seller] needs to consult an attorney or resort to litigation, including appellate proceedings, to enforce rights under this contract, then [Buyer or Seller] shall be entitled recover reasonable attorneys' fees and costs

Note:
Clause #3 is extra strong in that it also allows attorney fees if a party just calls his attorney for advice, and it only allows attorney fees to one side. However, even if the other party signs this a court might say that it applies to the other side as well. It might intimidate a party who doesn't use an attorney, but if it does go to court it might make the judge think the party who supplied the contract was the "bad guy."

Clause #4:
In the event of any dispute under this agreement, the parties agree to binding arbitration in accordance with the rules of the American Arbitration Association.

BROKER'S FEE

Buyer's View: Usually the seller is the only one who has contracted with a real estate broker and the buyer is not concerned with this agreement. If the buyer has a buyer's broker there is probably a contract spelling out that agreement. The buyer's broker might want his fee spelled out in the contract and paid to him at closing.

Seller's View: If the seller has some reason for disputing a broker's participation in the transaction, he would not want to acknowledge any participation by the broker in the sales contract. Therefore he would prefer that the commission not be mentioned in the contract. Since he presumably already has an agreement with the broker, there would be no need to repeat the terms of that agreement in the contract. However, if the broker's commission is undisputed it doesn't make much difference if it is in the contract.

Clause: [PREFER NO CLAUSE]

Broker's View: The broker would like it to be acknowledged in the contract that he was the procuring cause of the sale. When this is signed by both sides it may make it easier for the broker to collect if there is a dispute. The broker might not want the amount of his commission disclosed in the contract and prefer to say that the commission is "in accordance with the listing agreement between Seller and Broker."

Clause #1: Seller agrees to pay the registered real estate Broker named below, at the time of closing, from the disbursement of the proceeds of sale, compensation in the amount of _____% of gross purchase price or $_____ for his services in effecting the sale by finding a Buyer ready, willing, and able to purchase pursuant to the foregoing Contract. In the event Buyer fails to perform and deposit(s) are retained, 50% thereof, but not exceeding the Broker's commission above computed, shall be paid to the Broker as full consideration for Broker's services including costs expended by Broker, and the balance shall be paid to Seller. If the transaction shall not be closed by reason of refusal or failure of Seller to perform, the Seller shall pay said fee in full to Broker on demand.

Clause #2: Seller and Buyer acknowledge that Broker is the procuring cause of this Contract and Seller agrees to pay the registered real estate Broker named below, at the time of closing, from the disbursement of the proceeds of sale, compensation in the amount of _____% of gross purchase price or $_____ for his services in effecting the sale by finding a Buyer ready, willing, and able to purchase pursuant to the foregoing Contract. In the event Buyer fails to perform and deposit(s) are retained, 50% thereof, but not exceeding the Broker's commission above computed, shall be paid to the Broker as full consideration for Broker's services including costs expended by Broker, and the balance shall be paid to Seller. If the transaction shall not be closed by reason of refusal or failure of Seller to perform, the Seller shall pay said fee in full to Broker on demand.

Clause #3:

Seller and Buyer acknowledge that Broker is the procuring cause of this Contract and seller agrees to pay the registered real estate Broker named below, at the time of closing, from the disbursement of the proceeds of sale, compensation in accordance with the listing agreement between Seller and Broker, for his services in effecting the sale by finding a Buyer ready, willing, and able to purchase pursuant to the foregoing Contract. In the event Buyer fails to perform and deposit(s) are retained, 50% thereof, but not exceeding the Broker's commission above computed, shall be paid to the Broker as full consideration for Broker's services including costs expended by Broker, and the balance shall be paid to Seller. If the transaction shall not be closed by reason of refusal or failure of Seller to perform, the Seller shall pay said fee in full to Broker on demand.

CLOSING DATE AND PLACE

Definition: In different areas of the country the act of signing the final paperwork and finalizing the deal is called the **closing,** the **settlement** or the **escrow.** In the clauses on this page the proper term for your location should be used.

Buyer's View: The buyer wants the closing to be held at a time and place most convenient to him.

Clause #1:   Closing shall be on _____, 19___ at a location to be selected by Buyer.

Clause #2:   Closing shall be on _____, 19___ at _____.

Clause #3:   Closing shall be on _____, 19___ at _____. Time is of the essence of this Contract.

Seller's View: The seller wants the closing to be at a time and place most convenient to him.

Clause #1:   Closing shall be on _____, 19___ at the office of an attorney or closing agent designated by Seller.

Clause #2:   Closing shall be on _____, 19___ at the office of an attorney or closing agent selected by Seller. Time is of the essence of this Contract.

Note: If "time is of the essence" is used in a contract then the dates and times must be complied with strictly. If a party is late then the other party can declare the contract in default and back out of the deal. Where a party wants the deal to go through, even if it takes a little longer, this clause is not necessary.

Buyer's View: Buyer wants to be sure the Declaration of Condominium is satisfactory. Condominiums have all sorts of rules, some of which you might not expect. Some of them control the color of your draperies, whether or not you can enclose your porch, where you can park, what you can park on the property, how long you can have guests stay at your apartment, and many other aspects of daily life. If you cannot abide by these rules you should not buy in such developments.

People who have problems with their association over matters such as these often feel that their rights are being violated. But the rights of the owners have been determined before anyone buys in the complex, so it is important that you learn what these rules are before you sign a contract to buy.

Clause #1: If this property is a condominium, Buyer shall be given a copy of the Declaration of Condominium and all Amendments and rules and regulations promulgated thereunder within five days of acceptance of this Contract. Buyer shall have the option to cancel this Contract if said documents are not satisfactory to Buyer's needs.

Clause #2: If this property is a condominium, sale is contingent upon Buyer's attorney approving the Declaration of Condominium and all Amendments thereto and any rules and regulations promulgated thereunder.

Clause #3: If this property is a condominium, sale is contingent upon Buyer being able to use the property for ___Rental property and for___ ___storage of a boat.___

Note: Clause #1 gives the buyer the right to cancel the purchase for any reason. Therefore a court might hold that contract was not binding and that the seller also had the right to back out. Clause #2 might have a better chance of being held to be binding since it could be argued that the attorney must give an objective opinion. Clause #3 would be most likely to constitute a binding contract since it only allows the contract to be cancelled upon a certain condition.

Seller's View: Seller wants to sell the property as is with no contingencies.

Clause: [NO CLAUSE NECESSARY- See Restrictions & Easements Clause]

Buyer's View: Buyer wants to be sure to receive all Condominium rights and to have his deposit returned if the sale is not approved. He would also like to have the seller pay the costs of approval, if necessary, and for any improvements substantially completed.

Clause: If this property is a condominium, Seller shall convey all rights therein including common elements and limited common elements such as parking spaces and cabanas, if any. This Contract is contingent upon approval by the association or developer, if required, and Seller shall pay all costs of approval and transfer. Any assessments to be levied for work, improvements or services, which are substantially completed at time of closing, shall be paid by Seller.

Neutral Clause: If this property is a condominium, Seller shall convey all rights therein including common elements such as parking spaces and cabanas, if any. This contract is contingent upon the approval by the association or developer, if required, and the parties shall equally pay all costs of approval and transfer. Any assessments shall be prorated as of closing.

Seller's View: Seller wants Buyer to pay costs of approval and as much of the assessment fees as possible.

Clause: If this property is a condominium requiring approval by the association or developer, Buyer shall make application for approval within five days of acceptance of this Contract and shall pay all approval and transfer fees. Any assessments shall be prorated as of closing.

DEFAULT

Buyer's View: The buyer will hopefully have enough contingencies to avoid a default, but in the event he does default he wants his liability to be as low as possible. If the seller defaults he wants the choice of specific performance or monetary damages. The buyer should put down as small a deposit as possible.

Clause #1:   In the event Buyer defaults hereunder, Seller shall be entitled to the earnest money deposited herewith as liquidated damages. In the event Seller defaults hereunder, Buyer may proceed at law or in equity to enforce his rights under this contract.

Clause #2:   In the event Buyer defaults hereunder, Seller shall be entitled to his actual out-of-pocket expenses, and the Buyer shall have no further liability. The deposit paid under this Contract shall be returned to Buyer on demand. Buyer shall have no liability for commissions to any broker involved in this transaction. In the event Buyer must take legal action to recover the deposit, Seller shall be liable for Buyer's attorney's fees.

Neutral Clause: If the Buyer fails to perform under this Contract within the time specified, the deposit(s) paid by the Buyer may be retained by the Seller as liquidated damages, consideration for the execution of this Contract and full settlement of any claims, whereupon all parties shall be relieved of all obligations under this Contract. If, for any reason other than failure of Seller to render his title marketable after diligent effort, Seller fails, neglects, or refuses to perform under this Contract, Buyer may proceed at law or in equity to enforce his rights under this Contract.

Seller's View: The seller wants to keep the buyer's deposit plus any other damages or to be able to force the buyer to perform and wants to limit his liability in case he defaults. The seller should require as large a deposit as possible.

Clause: In the event Buyer defaults hereunder, Seller shall be entitled to retain any deposits paid hereunder as liquidated damages, or at his option, Seller may proceed to enforce specific performance of this Contract. In the event Seller defaults hereunder, Buyer shall be entitled to the sum of $_____ as liquidated damages from the Seller plus return of Buyer's deposit, if any.

Comment: Some contracts offer either the buyer or seller a choice of choosing between actual or liquidated damages. However, some courts have held such clauses unenforceable.

ENGINEERING REPORTS

Buyer's View: If the Buyer is purchasing land in order to build something on it, he wants to be sure that the land is suitable for his project. This may require tests of the soil, water table, bedrock, etc.

Clause #1: Contingent upon satisfactory engineering reports on the property for the building of a _____ as proposed by Buyer.

Clause #2: Contingent upon Buyer obtaining engineering reports on the property satisfactory to Buyer's contractor.

Seller's View: Seller prefers no contingencies in the deal.

Clause: (PREFER NO CLAUSE)

ENVIRONMENTAL CONDITIONS

Explanation: As explained in Chapter 6 an owner of property can be liable for any cleanup on the property.

Buyer's View: The buyer wants to protect himself from potential liability for cleanup of environmental hazards on the property. A *wise* seller would not guarantee that the problems had no problems because there might be some he doesn't know about,, but if the buyer can get such a clause accepted, and there is a "Survival of Contract" clause, the buyer may be able to sue the seller years later if anything turns up.

Clause: Seller warrants that the property is not in violation of any federal, state or local environmental laws.

Seller's View: The seller does not want to make any warranties as to the condition of the property. He may want to put in a clause relieving himself of potential liability. The first sentence of Clause #2 (below) should not be used if the seller has knowledge of any hazards. If the seller suspects that there might be a hidden problem he might not want to use either Clause #2 because if anything is detected the seller will be informed of and may then be unable to sell the property without paying for the cleanup.

Warning: If a seller thinks an environmental audit may uncover something, he may not want to have one done. Once the seller learns about a hazardous condition he must disclose it potential buyers and in some cases report it to governmental authorities. It may be possible to keep the audit confidential by hiring a lawyer to render confidential legal advice regarding the property. If the attorney orders the audit, the matter might be kept confidential by claiming attorney-client privilege. *Seek the advice of an attorney is such matters.*

Clause #1:   [PREFER NO CLAUSE]

Clause #2:   Seller is unaware of any environmental hazards on the property. Buyer shall have the right to have the property inspected for environmental factors within 15 days of acceptance of this contract. If Buyer is not satisfied with the environmental audit, Buyer may cancel this contract. If Buyer does not conduct an audit or cancel the contract within said 15 days then this right shall be waived and Buyer shall take the property as is.

EXISTING MORTGAGES

Buyer's View: The buyer needs to know all terms of the existing mortgage and wants to pay as little as possible to take over the loan. He would prefer to take the property subject to the mortgage, rather than assuming it, because if he assumes it he is personally liable to pay it in the event of a foreclosure. He would also like to have the seller pay the assumption fees and to give away his escrow balance, though the latter is very unlikely to be acceptable.

Clause #1:   Seller represents to Buyer that the existing mortgage on the property is held by _____ and bears interest at _____% per annum with monthly payments of $_____ principal and interest plus $_____ for escrow. Said loan is fully assumable under the following terms:_____
_____
_____.

Clause #2:   Seller represents to Buyer that the existing mortgage on the property is held by _____ and bears interest at _____% per annum with monthly payments of $_____ principal and interest plus $_____ for escrow. Said loan is fully assumable under the following terms:_____
_____
_____.
Seller to pay all costs of assumption and to bring current and transfer escrow balance, if any, without additional compensation. Said balance has been calculated into the purchase price.

Neutral Clause: Seller represents to Buyer that the existing mortgage on the property is held by _____ and bears interest at _____% per annum with monthly payment of $_____ principal and interest plus $_____ for escrow. Said loan is fully assumable under the following terms: _____
_____.

Seller's View: The buyer should assume the existing mortgage at whatever its terms, at the buyer's expense and should also protect the seller from future liability on the loan. For FHA and VA loans the seller should check into the procedures for being released and having eligibility restored.

Clause: Buyer to assume and hold Seller harmless on Mortgage to _____. Buyer to pay all costs of assumption and to purchase Seller's escrow balance, if any.

EXPENSES

Buyer's View:	The buyer wants to pay as few expenses as possible even if it is "customary" for him to pay them.
Clause #1:	Seller shall pay all closing costs, including all documentary stamps, transfer fees on the deed and mortgage, survey, termite report and appraisals.
Clause #2:	Seller shall pay for the documentary stamps or transfer taxes on the deed, costs of obtaining and recording any corrective instruments and for any intangible tax and recording of any mortgages to be executed by Buyer.
Clause #3:	Seller shall pay for the documentary stamps or transfer taxes on the deed, costs of obtaining and recording any corrective instruments and for any intangible tax and recording of any mortgages to Seller.
Comments:	Clause #1 is rarely acceptable to sellers; Clause #3 is standard in some areas which have intangible taxes on mortgages; Clause #2 requires the seller to pay the intangible tax and recording fee even if the mortgagee is a bank.
Neutral Clause:	The parties herein shall each pay half of the fees and costs for documentary stamps and transfer and recording fees.
Seller's View:	The seller wants to pay as few expenses as possible even if it is "customary" for the seller to pay them.
Clause #1:	Buyer shall pay all closing costs, including documentary stamps, transfer fees, survey, termite report and appraisals.
Clause #2:	Buyer shall pay for all closing costs, documentary stamps and transfer fees.
Note:	In different localities it may be customary for one or the other party to pay certain fees. Thus, where it is customary for a buyer to pay all of the fees, the neutral clause would cause an extra expense for the seller.

FINANCING CONTINGENCY

Buyer's View: The buyer wants to have his deposit refunded if he cannot obtain a suitable loan. Without this clause the buyer whose loan application is denied will lose his deposit. It is important to list the terms of the loan the buyer is seeking. Otherwise, if interest rates go up, the payments could be a lot more than expected and he may not want to go through with the purchase.

Clause: Contingent upon Buyer obtaining a mortgage loan for a minimum of $_____ at a maximum interest rate of _____% with payments not to exceed $_____ per month and no more that $_____ in loan points and fees. If Buyer is unable to obtain said loan prior to closing, Buyer's entire earnest money deposit shall be refunded immediately.

Neutral Clause: Contingent upon Buyer obtaining a firm commitment for a loan of at least $_____, at a maximum interest rate _____%, for a term of at least _____ years. Buyer agrees to make application for and use reasonable diligence to obtain said loan.

Seller's View: The seller wants a contract with no contingencies, but if financing is necessary, he wants to know as soon as possible if the loan will be approved.

Clause: Contingent upon Buyer obtaining a firm commitment within ____ days from acceptance for a loan of at least $_____. Buyer to make application within five days and use reasonable diligence to obtain said loan. Should Buyer fail to obtain said commitment or to waive this contingency within said time, either party may cancel this Contract.

INGRESS AND EGRESS

Buyer's View: The buyer wants to be sure there is legal access to the property and that he has a right to continued use of the access. In a platted subdivision this is not usually necessary, but when purchasing unplatted land it is very important.

Clause: Seller warrants that there is ingress and egress to the property which is insurable by a title insurance underwriter.

Comments: If the title policy or abstract indicates that there is no legal ingress and egress, the buyer probably will want to cancel the deal or require the seller to acquire ingress and egress rights prior to closing.

Seller's View: The seller doesn't care if there is legal ingress or egress; he just wants to sell the property. If the seller has a survey or title policy showing ingress and egress the above clause is acceptable. If seller doesn't know if there is legal ingress and egress he should not use the above warranty clause. If the buyer does not bring it up then no clause is necessary.

Clause: Property is being sold in "as is" condition with no representations or warranties of any nature being given by Seller.

INSPECTION

Buyer's View: The buyer wants to examine the property immediately before closing to be sure the property is in good condition and the contract is complied with.

Clause #1: Buyer shall be allowed to inspect the property within 24 hours of closing and at such time the Seller shall have the electrical service, water and gas on.

Clause #2: Contingent upon satisfactory inspection of the premises by a licensed contractor.

Comment: When the property is vacant and Buyer is moving in at closing, Buyer may want to turn water and power on in his name for the inspection. However, if Buyer will rent the property out, Buyer will not want to pay the expenses of putting the accounts in his name for a day and then into a tenant's name, so it is best to have the Seller pay for this.

Seller's View: The seller wants the buyer to take the property in its present condition.

Clause #1: Property is being sold in "as is" condition with no representations or warranties of any nature being given by Seller. Buyer has personally fully inspected the property, finds it satisfactory and does not rely on any representations not contained in this Contract.

Clause #2: Major appliances, heating, cooling, electrical and plumbing systems to be in working order as of six days prior to closing. Buyer may, at his expense, have inspections made of said items by licensed persons dealing in the repair and maintenance thereof, and shall report in writing to Seller such items as found not in working condition prior to taking possession thereof, or six days prior to closing, whichever occurs first. Unless Buyer reports failures by said date, he shall be deemed to have waived Seller's warranty as to failures not reported. Valid reported failures shall be corrected at Seller's cost. Seller agrees to provide access for inspection upon reasonable notice.

Note: This is the same clause as seller Clause #2 under Plumbing and Electrical.

INVESTMENT

Explanation: In some areas those who are buying property for investment, especially for a quick profit, must disclose this to the seller. This is especially true for those who hold real estate licenses. It is a violation of real estate licensing laws in some states not to disclose that one holds such a license. In some areas certain language may be required. If you are getting an especially good price on a property and think someone might later question the transaction, you might want to consider using clause #3.

Clause #1:   Buyer is a licensed real estate agent buying this property for investment.

Clause #2:   Buyer is a licensed real estate broker buying this property for investment.

Clause #3:   Buyer is a professional real estate investor buying this property for investment.

LEASES

Buyer's View: If the property is presently leased to someone, the buyer wants to be sure that leases on the property are reasonable and are assigned to him. The buyer may not want the property if it is subject to long leases at low rentals (such as a five year lease to the seller's brother at half the market rent).

Clause #1:   Contingent upon Buyer's approval of all leases affecting the property, copies of which shall be provided to Buyer five days after acceptance hereof. Prior to closing Seller shall furnish to Buyer estoppel letters from all tenants stating the nature and duration of occupancy, rental terms and any advanced rent and security deposits. In the event Seller is unable to obtain such letters, said information shall be furnished by Seller to Buyer in the form of a Seller's Affidavit and Buyer may thereafter contact tenants to confirm such information. Seller shall deliver and assign to Buyer all original leases at closing along with an assignment of all leases.

Clause #2:   Contingent upon Seller providing to Buyer proof that all leases are as represented to Buyer, and delivering to Buyer copies of all existing leases.

Seller's View: The buyer should take the property subject to all of the terms of the existing leases.

Clause: Property to be conveyed subject to existing leases, if any.

LIEN AFFIDAVIT

Buyer's View: The buyer wants the seller to provide an affidavit at closing stating that there are no liens on the property. This will usually be required by the closing agent and often includes such bills as for water, sewer, etc.

Clause: Seller shall, as to both the real and personal property being sold hereunder, furnish to Buyer at time of closing an affidavit attesting to the absence, unless otherwise provided for herein, of any financing statements, claims of lien or potential lienors known to Seller, and further attesting that there have been no improvements to the property for 90 days immediately preceding the date of closing. If the property has been improved within said time Seller shall deliver releases or waivers of all mechanic's liens, executed by general contractors, subcontractors, suppliers and materialmen, in addition to Seller's lien affidavit, setting forth the names of all such parties and further reciting that in fact all bills for work to the property which could serve as a basis for a mechanic's lien have been paid or will be paid at closing.

Seller's View: The seller gains nothing by the above clause, but need not object to it. If there are hidden claims against the property the seller would probably be sued if the buyer has to pay them.

Clause: [PREFER NO CLAUSE]

MAINTENANCE

Buyer's View: Buyer wants property in the best possible shape at closing.

Clause: Seller agrees to deliver the premises in good condition. Until possession seller shall maintain the property, including the lawn and shrubbery, and the pool, if any, shall be clean and clear. All floors to be washed or vacuumed and all walls to be clean and free of holes or damage.

Comment: With the above clause the buyer could argue for a slight reduction in the purchase price at the closing table if the property has not been cleaned and maintained.

Seller's View: The seller wants to convey the property as is.

Clause: Property is being sold in "as is" condition with no representations or warranties of any nature being given by Seller.

PERSONAL PROPERTY

Buyer's View:	The buyer wants to know which personal property is included in the purchase and to have it in working order.
Clause #1:	This sale includes all personal property listed on Schedule A plus any additional items remaining on the premises after closing. Seller warrants all items to be in working order at time of closing. (A "Schedule A" form is included with the forms in this book.)
Clause #2:	The following personal property is included in the purchase price: Range___ Oven___ Refrigerator___ Freezer___ Dishwasher___ Disposal___ Microwave___ Washer___ Dryer___ Heating System___ Air System___ Air Units___ Water Heater___ Water Softener___ Dehumidifier___ Ceiling Fans___ Pool Equipment___ Fireplace Equipment___ Swing Set___ Barbecue___ Curtains___ Drapes___ Rods___ Blinds___ Other_____ _____.
	plus all additional items remaining on the premises after closing. The parties agree that the portion of the purchase price attributable to the above items is $_____. Seller warrants all items to be in working order at time of closing.
Comment:	If the seller forgets his gold watch on a shelf, under clause #2 the buyer gets to keep it. Buyers of rental property would want the portion of the purchase price attributable to personal property as high as possible since it can be depreciated more quickly. See the Allocation of Purchase Price clauses.
Seller's View:	Seller doesn't want to warrant condition of the property or to include any items he didn't intend to sell.
Clause:	The following personal property is included in the purchase price and sold in "as is" condition: _____ _____.
Comment:	With this clause, if the seller forgot something on the premises he could assert that it was not included in the deal. If the property is being used as a rental (rather than a residence) the seller would not want to attribute much of the price to the personal property because he would probably have to pay tax on the depreciation recapture.

PLUMBING AND ELECTRICAL

Buyer's View: Buyer wants property in the best possible condition at time of closing with corrections made at the seller's expense.

Clause #1:   Seller warrants all heating, cooling, electrical and plumbing systems to be in working condition as of closing. Buyer may have inspections made of said systems by licensed persons dealing in the repair and maintenance thereof. All plumbing to be free from drips or leaks and in conformance with applicable standards, including septic system, if any, and all electrical fixtures to be in working order, including bulbs.

Clause #2:   Seller warrants all heating, cooling, electrical and plumbing systems to be in working condition as of closing.

Seller's View: Seller wants the buyer to take the property in its present condition.

Clause #1:   Property is being sold in "as is" condition with no representations or warranties of any nature being given by Seller.

Clause #2:   Major appliances, heating, cooling, electrical and plumbing systems to be in working order as of six days prior to closing. Buyer may, at his expense, have inspections made of said items by licensed persons dealing in the repair and maintenance thereof, and shall report in writing to Seller such items as found not in working condition prior to taking possession thereof, or six days prior to closing, whichever occurs first. Unless Buyer reports failures by said date, he shall be deemed to have waived Seller's warranty as to failures not reported. Valid reported failures shall be corrected at Seller's cost. Seller agrees to provide access for inspection upon reasonable notice.

Comments: If the buyer insists upon warranties, Clause #2 makes sure they are taken care of or waived before closing.

POSSESSION

Buyer's View: The buyer wants possession of the property at closing or compensation for any delays. The figures in the following clauses are for illustration. The may need to be higher or may be negotiated lower.

Clause #1:   Seller shall deliver exclusive possession of the premises to Buyer at closing subject only to leases assigned to Buyer which are current in rent. In the event any rents are in arrears, the sum of $500.00 of Seller's funds shall be held in escrow by closing agent for each unit in arrears, to cover costs of eviction and lost rent, if any. If Seller is to remain in possession of the property at closing, Seller's proceeds shall not be released until Seller has fully vacated the property, and Buyer shall be entitled to $50.00 per day for each day Seller holds over.

Clause #2:   Seller shall deliver exclusive possession of the premises to Buyer at closing subject only to leases assigned to Buyer which are paid current.

Comments: In the above clauses "leases" can also include oral leases.

Seller's View: The seller wants the buyer to take the property subject to existing tenancies, if any, and to not pay any penalties if he is to stay after closing.

Clause :   Possession shall be delivered at closing subject to existing tenancies, if any.

PRORATIONS

Buyer's View: Buyer wants full credits from the seller for all taxes owed and rents and security deposits prepaid.

Clause #1:   Taxes, rents, interest, property owner dues, insurance acceptable to Buyer and _____ shall be prorated as of closing. Any security deposits shall be turned over to Buyer.

Clause #2:   Taxes, rents, interest, property owner dues, and insurance acceptable to Buyer and _____ shall be prorated as of closing. Real and personal property taxes shall be prorated based upon the most recent available information. If closing occurs at a date when the current year's millage is not fixed, and current year's assessment is available, taxes will be prorated based upon such assessment and the prior year's millage. If current year's assessment is not available, then taxes will be prorated on the prior year's tax; provided, however, if there are improvements on the property completed by January 1st of the year of closing, which improvements were not in existence on January 1st of the prior year, then taxes shall be prorated based upon the prior year's millage and at an equitable assessment to be agreed upon between the parties, failing which, request will be made to the property appraiser or assessor for an informal assessment. Any tax proration based upon an estimate may, at the request of Buyer, be subsequently readjusted upon receipt of the tax bill. Prepaid rents and other tenant deposits shall be prorated to the date of closing. Any security deposits shall be turned over to Buyer.

Seller's View: The seller would prefer the buyer to take title subject to taxes and without rent credits. But if prorated, the seller would prefer the lowest figures be used with no possibility for future obligations.

Clause #1:   Neither taxes nor rents shall be prorated as these amounts have been calculated into the sales price.

Clause #2:   Real and personal property taxes shall be prorated according to the last available bill and no future adjustments shall be required. Rents and other tenant deposits shall be prorated as of the date of closing.

Note: Before deciding which clause is best you must first figure out if the proration would cost you money or give you extra money. In some areas taxes may be assessed or collected a year or two in advance or in arrears. This would make a difference in the which clause works best.

PURCHASE MONEY MORTGAGES

Note: In some areas a "deed of trust" is used instead of a mortgage.

Buyer's View: The buyer wants the best terms on the mortgage to save him money and lessen his risk of default. Most important are a long grace period on late payments and the right to have the mortgage assumed by a later buyer, but some buyers like to ask for a lot more. This clause is one of the most important in the contract and could result in tens of thousands of dollars in additional profit.

Clause #1:   In the event Seller will hold a purchase money mortgage under this Contract, said mortgage shall contain no prepayment penalty, be fully assumable and allow a 60-day grace period on late payments. Mortgagee shall look only to the collateral for security and not be entitled to any deficiency judgment. Mortgagor shall have a first right of refusal at any time mortgagee desires to sell the note and mortgage at a discount, and mortgagor may have parts of the property released from the mortgage proportional to the principal paid. Mortgagor shall be permitted to miss one monthly payment per loan year without default and shall be able to substitute other collateral of equal equity value at any time.

Clause #2:   In the event Seller will hold a purchase money mortgage under this contract, said mortgage shall contain no prepayment penalty, be fully assumable and allow a 30-day grace period on late payments. Mortgagor shall have a first right of refusal at any time mortgagee desires to sell the note and mortgage at a discount.

Comments: Few sellers would accept all of the provisions in Clause #1, but some of them may be accepted.

Seller's View: The seller wants a non-assumable mortgage with a lot of protective clauses.

Clause #1:   In the event Seller will hold a purchase money mortgage under this Contract said mortgage will be on a standard form used by lenders in the area and contain a "due on sale clause."

Clause #2:   In the event Seller will hold a purchase money mortgage under this Contract said mortgage shall contain a 10-day grace period and provide that if any interest in the property is transferred (other than a subordinate lien or lease without an option) the interest rate shall be adjusted upward to the average fixed loan rate at the following institutions _____.

RADON CLAUSE

Explanation: The recent discovery that radon gas is present in many homes and is a health hazard is causing new laws and regulations to be passed around the country. This, of course, is resulting in new lawsuits and attempts to find liability. Since the issue is so new there is no way to know what laws will be passed or which contract clauses will hold up the best. However, the following suggestions may be helpful.

Buyer's View: If the property is in a high-radon area, the buyer may want to have a radon test done on the house. He would prefer to have the seller pay for it and would like to back out of the deal if the house is found to have high levels of radon.

Clause #1: Seller, at his expense, shall provide Buyer at least 15 days prior to closing with a report by a licensed inspector acceptable to Buyer, of the level of radon gas in the premises. In the event levels of radon gas are unacceptable to Buyer, Buyer may cancel this Contract.

Clause #2: Seller, at his expense, shall provide Buyer at least 15 days prior to closing with a report by a licensed inspector acceptable to Buyer, of the level of radon gas in the premises. In the event levels of radon gas are unacceptable to Buyer, Buyer may cancel this Contract or require that radon gas reduction equipment be installed on the property at Seller's expense, not to exceed 3% of the purchase price.

Note: There are not yet clear standards as to what amount of radon is acceptable. Therefore these clauses allow the buyer to back out if any is found or to accept the property if minor amounts are found and mitigation equipment is installed.

Seller's View: The Seller wants to sell the property without any delays or expenses due to radon problems. Therefore the less said about the issue the better. Because sellers have been held liable for not disclosing known defects in their properties, a seller might not want to voluntarily have a radon test done if it was not requested.

Florida Clause: A law in Florida requires the following clause in all contracts for sale (and lease) or real property. This law may be beneficial to sellers in that by giving a warning to buyers, they may be protected from liability if radon is found later.

RADON GAS: Radon is a naturally occurring radioactive gas that, when it has accumulated in a building in sufficient quantities, may present health risks to persons who are exposed to it over time. Levels of radon that exceed federal and state guidelines have been found in buildings in Florida. Additional information regarding radon and radon testing may be obtained from your county public health unit.

Other States:

Persons in areas other than Florida should check to see if any new laws have been passed in their area. (Boards of Realtors should know.) If no clause is required, the Florida clause could be used by changing the state name and may offer some protection.

RECORDING

Buyer's View: Buyer would like to record the contract to protect his interest if Seller refuses to close.

Clause: [No clause necessary, but be sure contract has correct legal description and that Seller's signatures are notarized.]

Seller's View: Seller does not want contract recorded to cloud his title to the property. Seller should not allow his signature to be notarized.

Clause: Neither this Contract nor any notice of it shall be recorded in any public records.

RESTRICTIONS AND EASEMENTS

Buyer's View: The buyer does not want to buy property if restrictions or easements prohibit his intended use of the property or adversely affect its value

Most restrictions add to the value of the property by forbidding neighbors from doing obnoxious things like having clotheslines or trucks in the front yard. However, if a buyer wants to install a six foot fence or a pool and restrictions don't allow it, he probably doesn't want the property. Some restrictions forbid parking cars on the street or control the color that the house may be painted. Be sure to check these things before closing.

Clause #1:   Sale contingent upon property being free and clear of any easements or restrictions which adversely affect the value of the property to Buyer.

Clause #2:   Sale contingent upon property being free and clear of any easements or restrictions which adversely affect the value of the property to Buyer. Seller to provide Buyer with copies of all applicable restrictions and easements at least 15 days prior to closing.

Seller's View: The seller wants the buyer to buy the property as is.

Clause: Property to be conveyed subject to easements, covenants and restrictions of record.

RISK OF LOSS

Buyer's View: In the event part of the premises are destroyed before closing, buyer may want to take the property as is with an assignment of the insurance proceeds or to cancel the contract.

Clause: If the improvements are damaged by fire or other casualty prior to closing, Buyer shall have the option of either taking the property as is together with the insurance proceeds available by virtue of such loss or damage, or of cancelling this Contract and receiving return of deposit(s) made hereunder.

Neutral Clause: If the improvements are damaged by fire or other casualty prior to closing, and the cost of restoring same does not exceed 3% of the assessed valuation of the improvements so damaged, Buyer shall have the option of either taking the property as is, together with either the said 3% or any insurance proceeds payable by virtue of such loss or damage, or of cancelling this Contract and receiving return of deposit(s) made hereunder.

Seller's View: In the event part of the premises are destroyed before closing the seller may want to cancel the contract and keep the insurance proceeds and the property, or he may prefer to repair the premises and continue with the closing.

Clause: If the improvements are damaged by fire or other casualty prior to closing, Seller may cancel this Contract, or may extend the closing date up to 90 days and restore the premises to substantially their original condition.

ROOF CLAUSE

Buyer's View: Buyer wants roof to be in as good condition as possible at the seller's expense. Some mortgage lenders require such an inspection.

Clause #1:   The Seller, within the time allowed for delivery of evidence of title and examination thereof, or no later than ten days prior to closing, whichever date occurs last, shall have the roof inspected at Seller's expense by a licensed roofer, licensed general contractor or a firm specializing in presale inspections of property to determine that there is no visible evidence of leaks or damage (including facia and soffit.) If repairs are needed, Seller shall have them completed at his expense by a licensed roofer, or at Buyer's option shall credit the Buyer for the cost of said repairs.

Clause #2:   The Buyer, within the time allowed for delivery of evidence of title and examination thereof, or no later than ten days prior to closing, whichever date occurs last, may have the roof inspected at Buyer's expense by a licensed roofer, licensed general contractor or a firm specializing in presale inspections of property to determine that there is no visible evidence of leaks or damage (including facia and soffit.) If repairs are needed, Seller shall pay up to two percent of the purchase price for the repairs which shall be performed by a licensed roofer or licensed general contractor. If the cost of repairs exceeds two percent of the purchase price, Seller may cancel this Contract.

Seller's View: The seller wants the buyer to take the property in its present condition.

Clause: Property is being sold in "as is" condition with no representations or warranties of any nature being given by Seller.

SEVERABILITY

Explanation:

Occasionally a contract will be declared void by a court because of some clause in it which is found to be repugnant. To avoid the whole contract being thrown out because of one clause a severability clause is used. This clause says that the contract should not be declared void due to one part being invalid. However, if the invalid clause is an important part of the deal then the person presenting the contract might not want the contract to be upheld.

This clause would be needed in a contract which is drafted to favor one side very strongly.

Clause:

In the event any clause in this Contract is held to be unenforceable, or against public policy, such holding shall not affect the validity of the remainder of the Contract unless it materially alters the terms hereof.

SPECIAL ASSESSMENTS

Buyer's View: The buyer wants the seller to pay all special assessments levied and pending against the property.

Clause: Certified, confirmed and ratified special assessment liens as of date of closing (and not as of Contract date) are to be paid by Seller. Pending liens as of date of closing shall be assumed by Buyer, provided, however, that where the improvement has been substantially completed as of the date of closing, such pending liens shall be considered as certified, confirmed or ratified and Seller shall, at closing, be charged an amount equal to the last estimate by the public body making the assessment for the improvement.

Neutral Clause: Certified, confirmed and ratified special assessment liens as of date of closing (and not as of Contract date) are to be paid by Seller. Pending liens as of date of closing shall be assumed by Buyer.

Seller's View: In some cases the seller would want the buyer to take over assessment liens on the property, but in any case Seller wants to pay only assessments which are liens on the property as of closing.

Clause #1: Property is sold subject to assessments of record.

Clause #2: Seller shall be responsible only for assessments which appear as liens on the property as of the date of closing.

Comment: When using Clause #1, the seller should disclose assessments to the buyer.

SURVEY

Buyer's View: It is always best to have a survey of the property, but in a platted subdivision a new survey is not usually necessary unless a mortgage lender is requiring it or if the boundary of the property is uncertain. In many cases an old survey along with a title report is sufficient to show buyer where easements and boundaries are. When buying vacant land a survey is absolutely necessary. Some lots have easements running down the middle of them or have been found to be a block away from where the "For Sale" sign was located! Usually a buyer pays for the survey but a desperate or naive seller may agree to pay the cost.

Clause: Seller shall provide Buyer with a survey of the property certified within 30 days of closing. In the event encroachments are indicated they shall be corrected at the expense of Seller.

Seller's View: Seller has no need for a survey and if the buyer wants one he should pay for it. A survey may find problems which may delay the closing and be costly to the seller to correct.

Clause #1:   (NO CLAUSE NEEDED)

Clause #2:   Buyer may, at his expense and within 15 days of acceptance of this Contract, have the property surveyed by a licensed surveyor. In the event encroachments are indicated and brought to Seller's attention within said 15 days, Seller may correct them at his expense or cancel this Contract.

Note: In some areas a survey may be required by law.

SURVIVAL OF CONTRACT

Buyer's View: In some jurisdictions the contract of sale is considered to have "merged" into the deed once the closing has taken place. This means that any promises or warranties in the contract are deemed to have been waived if not fulfilled or otherwise put into another writing at closing. If there are any such provisions (such as "Seller warrants that the property is free of violations of government regulations," or "Seller will pay assessments") which will not be fulfilled at closing, this clause should be used. If this clause is not used, a separate agreement such as an escrow agreement can be executed at closing which will continue the obligations of the contract.

Clause #1: This Contract and the covenants herein shall survive the closing.

Clause #2: This Contract and all of its provisions shall not be extinguished by merger of the deed of bargain and sale, but shall expressly survive the transfer of the property.

Seller's View: In most cases the seller just wants his money with no further obligations or possible liabilities. Any continuing obligations of buyer are usually contained in the mortgage and note executed at closing.

Clause: [USUALLY PREFER NO CLAUSE]

TERMITES

Buyer's View:
The seller should deliver the premises free of wood-destroying organisms and pay for inspection and treatment. The buyer should have the option to back out of deal if infestation is discovered. The buyer would prefer that a major national company do the inspection because a small one might go out of business and not be available if it turns out that termites were missed by the inspector.

Clause #1:
Seller, at his expense, shall provide Buyer with a report by a certified pest control operator acceptable to Buyer, dated within 30 days of closing, that there are no signs of infestation by wood destroying organisms. In the event infestation is indicated, Buyer may cancel this Contract or the property shall be treated and repaired at the expense of Seller.

Clause #2:
Seller, at his expense, shall provide Buyer with a report by a certified pest control operator acceptable to Buyer, dated within 30 days of closing, that there are no signs of infestation by wood destroying organisms. In the event infestation is indicated, Buyer may cancel this Contract or the property shall be treated and repaired at the expense of Seller of up to 3% of the purchase price.

Neutral Clause:
Within 30 days of closing the premises shall be inspected by a certified Pest Control operator acceptable to Buyer and the cost of said inspection shall be paid equally by Buyer and Seller. In the event infestation by wood destroying organisms is indicated, either party may cancel this Contract or Seller may treat the premises at his expense.

Seller's View:
The seller wants to pay as little as possible and to cancel the deal if the cost of treatment is too high. Using a large national company to do the inspection could protect the buyer. If infestation is discovered later and the company which did the inspection is out of business the buyer might sue the seller.

Clause #1:
Property is sold in "as is" condition with no representations or warranties of any nature being given by Seller.

Clause #2:
Buyer may, at his expense, no less than 15 days before closing, have the improvements inspected by a licensed termite inspector. In the event active infestation is indicated, Seller shall have the option to treat the premises or cancel this Contract.

Note:
In some areas a termite inspection may be required by law.

TITLE DEFECTS

Buyer's View: The buyer wants the seller to cure any title defects promptly at the seller's expense or to be able to cancel the deal. In some cases it may require a lawsuit and a considerable amount of time to cure a title defect. If the property is an especially good deal the buyer may want to give the seller a longer period of time in which to cure. The buyer might also wish to take the property with the defect if he can get a reduction in price.

Clause: In the event title is found to be defective, Seller shall have 60 days within which to remove such defects. If Seller is unable to cure them within such time, Buyer may cancel this Contract and have all earnest money refunded or may allow Seller additional time to cure. Seller agrees to use diligent effort to correct the defects including the bringing of necessary suits.

Seller's View: The seller wants to be able to back out of the deal if the title report shows defects which are either too costly to cure. Since it may take some time to cure some defects, seller would like as much time as possible to cure them and still go through with the contract.

Clause #1:   In the event title is found defective, Buyer shall within three days thereafter notify Seller in writing specifying the defects or else same shall be waived. If defects render title unmarketable Seller shall have 120 days within which to cure said defects or to cancel this Contract.

Clause #2:   In the event title is found defective, Buyer shall within three days thereafter notify Seller in writing specifying the defects or else same shall be waived. If defects render title unmarketable Seller shall have 180 days within which to cure said defects or to cancel this Contract.

TITLE EVIDENCE

Buyer's View: The buyer wants to examine title as soon as possible at seller's expense.

Clause #1:   Within _____ days from acceptance of this Contract Seller shall, at his expense, provide to Buyer a title insurance commitment for a fee simple owner's marketable title policy in the amount of the purchase price, or if it is the prevailing custom in the locality, an abstract of title, to be paid for at closing by Seller.

Clause #2:   At least _____ days prior to closing Seller shall, at his expense, provide to Buyer a title insurance commitment for a fee simple owner's marketable title policy in the amount of the purchase price, or if it is the prevailing custom in the locality, an abstract of title, to be paid for by Seller at closing.

Neutral Clause: Seller shall purchase and deliver to Buyer at or before closing a title insurance policy, or if it is the prevailing custom in the locality, an abstract of title.

Seller's View: Seller would like buyer to pay for the title policy or abstract, but in many areas it is customary to charge this expense to seller unless buyer agrees to pay "all closing costs." If seller does pay he would not want to obtain the commitment for the title insurance policy until the last minute in case the deal falls through.

Clause #1:   (Same as neutral clause)

Clause #2:   Buyer may at his expense obtain a title insurance policy or abstract of title.

Note: In some areas a "Torrens" system is used in which a person gets a title certificate similar to a car title. It this is the case in your county you should substitute the appropriate wording.

VIOLATIONS

Buyer's View: The buyer does not want to find out after closing that the property is in violation of several codes and that thousands of dollars worth of repairs are needed. To be sure to be able to take advantage of this warranty a clause should be added stating that the contract survives the closing.

Clause #1: Seller warrants property to be free from violations of building, health and other governmental codes and ordinances.

Clause #2: Seller represents to Buyer that he has received no notice of violation on the property of any building, health or other governmental codes or ordinances.

Notes: Clause #1 would not usually be acceptable to a sophisticated seller since it even warrants that the property is free from violations that he doesn't know about.

Seller's View: Seller doesn't want to warrant anything.

Clause: Property is being sold in "as is" condition with no representations or warranties of any nature being given by Seller.

Comment: In some large cities the codes are so strict that all properties are in violation, but no one is cited unless he causes trouble for someone connected with the city government.

WATER ACCESS

Buyer's View: If the buyer is purchasing property purported to be "on the water" then he wants to be sure that it is actually on the water and that all possible water rights are included. Some properties appear to be waterfront but are actually landlocked by thin strips of land owned by strangers, and many docks are on state owned or privately owned bottom lands.

Clause: Seller warrants the property to have water access and to have riparian rights. Any dock appurtenant to the property is legally constructed and does not encroach upon any other property.

Seller's View: The seller doesn't want to warrant anything. He wants to sell whatever it is he owns and does not want to end up in a lawsuit if it is not what the buyer expected.

Clause: Property is being sold in "as is" condition with no representations or warranties of any nature being given by Seller.

WRAPAROUND AND SECOND MORTGAGES

Buyer's View: If the property has a first mortgage (deed of trust) and the seller will be financing some amount in addition to that, the buyer would prefer a second mortgage to a wraparound mortgage. This way the buyer can be sure the first mortgage is paid and possibly take advantage of an advantageous interest rate.

The problem with a wraparound mortgage is that the buyer can make payments to the seller for several months, while the seller pockets the money and lets the first mortgage go into default. If the buyer does agree to a wraparound mortgage, he wants clauses in it that protect him from the seller defaulting on the first mortgage.

Clause #1:   The mortgage held by Seller shall be a second mortgage and buyer shall take title to the property subject to the first mortgage.

Clause #2:   The mortgage held by Seller shall be a second mortgage and buyer shall assume the first mortgage.

Clause #3:   The wraparound mortgage held by Seller shall state that Seller must provide proof to Buyer of payment on the underlying mortgage(s) at least every _____ days. In the event Seller defaults in payment, Buyer may make payments and deduct any amounts so paid from payments due to Seller.

Seller's View: The seller's position is exactly the opposite of the buyer's. The seller would prefer a wraparound mortgage to a second mortgage so that he can be sure the first mortgage is being paid. A buyer could make payments on the second mortgage and let the first go into default resulting in a foreclosure and loss of the seller's interest.

If the seller does take back a second mortgage he wants clauses in it which protect him from the possibility of a default on the first mortgage by the buyer.

Clause #1:   The mortgage held by Seller shall be a wraparound mortgage.

Clause #2:   The mortgage held by Seller shall state that Buyer must provide proof to Seller of payments on the underlying mortgage(s) at least every _____ days. In the event Buyer defaults in payment, Seller may make up such payments, add such amounts to the balance of his mortgage and accelerate the balance of said mortgage.

ZONING AND ORDINANCES

Buyer's View: Buyer wants to back out of the contract if the zoning affecting the property will not permit him to use the property for his intended purpose.

Clause #1:   Contingent upon Buyer's ability to use the property for _____ _____.

Clause #2:   Contingent upon zoning and ordinances not affecting Buyer's intended use of the property.

Comments: In some cities there are laws, for example, which prohibit boats or RVs from being stored on the property or which prohibit parking on the street at night. If buyer has a boat or three cars he might not want such a property. Buyer should check local laws prior to closing.

Seller's View: Seller wants no contingencies.

Clause: Property to be conveyed subject to governmental zoning and ordinances.

Chapter 10
Creative Clauses

To really make a profit on a real estate deal you can use clauses which are more creative than the usual ones and which give you more flexibility.

Depending upon who you are dealing with, some of these clauses might be considered unfair if the case ever comes to court. Therefore you should consider using the "Severability Clause" with these and to read Chapter 7 on overreaching. Also, it is possible that in some jurisdictions some of these clauses may cause the transaction to be in violation of some law.

Interest on Deposit

Explanation: If the Buyer is putting down a large deposit for a property, he wants it to earn interest prior to closing, and to be credited with that interest.

Clause: The deposit hereunder shall be placed in an interest-bearing account with the interest credited to Buyer at closing.

Note as Deposit

Explanation: The Buyer does not want to tie up money before closing and he wants it to be difficult for the seller to take his deposit if he defaults.

Clause: Buyer's deposit under this contract shall consist of a promissory note payable in full at closing and bearing no interest.

Services as Down Payment

Explanation: A buyer who has no money to put down on a property might be able to make a deal to perform some services for the seller as the down payment.

Clause: The parties agree that in lieu of down payment in the amount of $_____ for this purchase, the Buyer shall perform the following services for the Seller on for before
_____:_____
_____.

Property as Down Payment

Explanation: A buyer who has no money to put down on a property might be able to make a deal to trade some other real or personal property as the down payment.

Clause: The parties agree that the down payment on this transaction shall be the following property which shall be transferred to Seller at closing and which is agreed to have a value of $_____:_____
_____.

Mortgage (Deed of Trust) as Down Payment

Explanation: A buyer who has no money to put down on a property might be able to place a mortgage (deed of trust) on another property he owns as the down payment.

Clause: The Buyer may, at his option, use as the down payment a note secured by a mortgage on his property located at _____.

Mortgage (Deed of Trust) Clauses

Explanation: When the seller will be taking back a mortgage, it is a good time to become creative. Such clauses can result in much greater profits on the property. The first clause is used when the property consists of separate units or tracts of land. It allows the buyer to own part of the property free and clear before the entire balance is paid.

Clause: At such time as the balance of the mortgage is $_____, buyer may have the following portion of the property released from the mortgage: _____

The following clause may prevent the buyer from losing the property in the event of financial hardship. The second sentence protects the seller but also helps the clause seem less onerous.

Clause: Buyer shall have the right to miss one loan payment in each calendar year without causing a default of the mortgage. Such missed payment shall not affect accrual of interest.

Exchange

Explanation: To avoid paying tax on the sale the seller may want to structure it as a tax-free exchange by locating another property and structuring the deal into a trade.

Clause: This contract is contingent upon Seller finding a suitable property which can be used to structure this transaction as an exchange under Section 1031 of the I. R. S. Code.

Credits

Explanation: When there are obvious problems with the property it may be possible to require them to be fixed or to get a lower price. Using this clause brings such flaws to the attention of the seller.

Clause: Unless the following items are repaired prior to closing, the buyer will be credited at closing for the amount listed opposite each item:

_____	$_____
_____	$_____
_____	$_____

Unpaid Rent

Explanation: If some of the rent from current tenants is past due the landlord would like to get it eventually. This is usually hopeless, but in some cases may be worthwhile. The seller could file a suit against the tenant after the closing or could require the buyer to collect the rents

Clause: If at the time of closing any of the rents on the premises are in arrears, Buyer shall collect such amounts and remit them to Seller as collected.

Examination of Books

Explanation: When purchasing large rental properties the buyer is usually interested in knowing how much money the property has produced for the seller. Therefore he needs to examine the seller's financial records as in buying any business.

Clause: Within 10 days of the acceptance of this agreement Seller shall deliver to Buyer his books and records of account for the property. Buyer shall have 15 days in which to examine them. If Buyer gives written notice within said 15 days that the property is not acceptable to him, then this contract shall be cancelled and Buyer's deposit returned.

F.H.A./V.A. Fees

Explanation: The buyer would like it if the seller would pay his loan fees. The seller probably won't but it can't hurt to ask. He might have figured enough profit into the price to cover them. Also, it is something for the buyer to give up in the next round. If a conventional loan is being sought this clause can be amended to cover points on that type of loan.

Clause: Seller shall pay any F.H.A. or V.A. points on the mortgage loan for this transaction.

Sale of Other Property

Explanation: In some cases the buyer will not be able to make the purchase until another property he owns is sold.

Clause: This contract is contingent upon the sale of Buyer's property at _____.
Closing of this contract shall be simultaneous with the closing of the sale of Buyer's property.

Perc Test

Explanation: If the buyer is buying land and intends to install a septic system he will want to be sure that the ground is absorbent enough to accommodate one. This is checked by doing a percolation test.

Clause: This contract is contingent upon the property passing a percolation test that meets the standards of the governmental agency having authority over such tests in the area.

Presentation of Contract

Explanation: Some real estate agents prefer to approach the seller alone to present the contract. In some cases the buyer would prefer to be present, such as when the agent might have another prospect or friend interested in the property.

Clause: This contract shall be presented to Seller in the presence of Buyer.

Distribution of Proceeds

Explanation: If the sellers are getting a divorce or dissolving a partnership they may want separate checks at the closing.

Clause: The net proceeds to the Seller at closing shall be distributed in separate checks as follows:

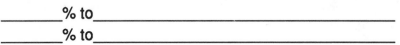

_____% to_____
_____% to_____

Chapter 11
Signing the Contract

Typically a contract for the sale of real estate contains several changes which must be accepted by each side before the contract is legally enforceable. Under basic contract law a contract must either be accepted as offered or any changes to it become a counteroffer. This counteroffer then must be accepted by the original offeror to create a binding contract. The contract is not binding until all of the changes have been accepted by all parties.

If a contract becomes messy and unreadable with numerous additions and deletions it is wise to redraft the contract including all changes and have it signed by all parties. Otherwise, one or more omitted initials can result in the contract being unenforceable.

At any point before all of the changes have been accepted by all parties, any of them can withdraw the offer and cancel the deal. For example, if you are negotiating to buy a house and have most of the terms worked out but the seller won't include the washer and dryer, if you then withdraw the offer the seller cannot then change his mind and force you to buy it with the washer and dryer included. The sellers late acceptance is really a new offer which you may accept or reject.

Before putting your final signature on the contract you should review the following checklist:

- Are all clauses in the contract worded correctly?
- Have you included all of the necessary contingencies to protect your interest?
- Have you read all of the fine print?
- Are all terms legible?
- Are all changes initialed?

• Is everything you assume or understand about the deal written in the contract?

• Does the contract contain the proper signatures of the other parties?

Witnesses

Some states do not require witnesses on contracts for the sale of real estate but it is always good to have them in case the issue goes to court. To find out the requirements in your state call a local real estate agent.

Notary

A real estate contract does not usually need to be notarized. From the seller's point of view it would be better if it were not notarized because a notarized contract could in most cases be recorded by the buyer, placing a cloud on the title to the property. The buyer's point of view is the opposite; the notarization may be helpful if the seller tries to back out of the deal.

PART THREE - AFTER SIGNING THE CONTRACT

Chapter 12
Backing Out of the Deal

As a general rule, once a real estate contract has been signed, both parties are bound to go through with it unless some contingency has not been met. There is no "three-day right of recision" and you can't legally get out of it by lying to the bank about your income.

However, most contracts are sloppily drawn and many have loopholes which allow escape. Because of the amount of money involved it is wise to seek the advice of an attorney who is experienced in real estate law before repudiating a contract. He or she may be able to point out clear reasons why you can or cannot get out of the contract.

You must realize, though, that the law is not always clear. Law books are full of cases where attorneys advised their clients they were in the right, but were proven wrong years and many thousands of dollars later.

In many cases the best thing to do is to present the problem to the other side or to your real estate agent. Perhaps they can amend the deal to solve whatever problem you have with it. Another thing to consider is that many people get second thoughts after a deal is finalized. For buyers its called "buyers' remorse" and it is usually not logical. The fear of having made such a big decision puts doubts in the buyers' minds and they find every reason for not going through with the deal. Its kind of like the fear some people get a week before their wedding day.

Many people with such fears overcome them and find their home was the best purchase they ever made. Others actually back out of the deal and end up spending more money in court than the deposit they put down. The best thing to do for buyers' remorse is to imagine that the seller wants to back out of the deal because he realizes that he's giving you too good a deal.

If you truly made a mistake, or had a change of circumstances which would make the transaction wrong for you, you may be able to get out of the deal. It usually depends upon whether you put any contingencies in the contract.

Contingencies

If you read this book carefully before signing the contract you should have put several contingencies in the contract. Many of these can let you out of the deal. The most common one is financing. Usually people exaggerate their financial condition. If you deflate your position to something more realistic, mentioning some contingent liabilities, you might be rejected for the loan. Clauses which call for approval by your spouse, partner or attorney can also give you an out.

Sellers

Sellers usually have a much harder time of getting out of the contract. However, if the contract is loose enough to let the buyer out easily, it may be unenforceable. Ask your lawyer if he or she could hire law student to spend a few hours finding the latest cases in your state on enforceability of real estate contracts.

Default

If you do refuse to go through with the deal, your penalty will be decided by the default clause you put in the contract. As a buyer you should have put in a clause saying that in the event of your default you lost only your deposit. You also should have put up only a small deposit, such as $100 or $500.

As a seller you should have put a similar clause in the contract. If you default the buyer gets a flat sum of, say, $500.

Attorneys' Fees

The most expensive thing about defaulting on a contract is the attorney fees. In most cases (depending on the clause in your contract) the loser pays both sides' attorneys' fees. If each side only spends 100 hours on the case the fees could easily be $20,000 to $30,000. Keep this in mind when deciding whether or not to breach the contract or to sue over the other side's breach.

Chapter 13
Rescuing the Deal

Some real estate deals close quickly and effortlessly. Others go from crisis to crisis for months and then fall apart completely. If yours looks like it is falling apart, don't give up. There are often ways to keep it on track.

One way to prevent the deal from falling through is to impress upon the other side that there will be a lawsuit if they do not go through with the deal. Once the party realizes that this may cost them tens of thousands of dollars and keep them in court for years, they may decide the problem with the contract is not worth it. Of course this argument can only be used when the contract is legally binding.

The following sections discuss some common problems and possible ways to solve them.

Financing

Probably the most common problem is the buyer not being able to qualify for the loan or being unable to come up with a large enough down payment. A few solutions are listed below. Some of them require more complicated actions than can be discussed here and some may be illegal if not done properly. If any of these seem to be able to help you, seek advice from your broker or attorney.

- Seller can loan buyer part of the down payment
- Seller can accept some personal or real property as part of the down payment
- Buyer can get a loan against other property he owns
- Buyer's parents can loan or give money to buyer
- Buyer's parents can co-sign on the loan
- Buyer's parents can qualify for the loan and add buyer's name to the property
- Parties can enter into a lease/option agreement until buyer builds up equity

Defects

If the buyer has properly drafted his contract, the sale will be contingent on the property not having major defects. If an expensive problem is discovered it is usually the duty of the seller to fix it or to lower the price. The seller may not want to go ahead with the deal if he has to pay for this.

If the seller has properly negotiated the contract he will be able to back out of the deal if repairs are too expensive. If the buyer prevailed the seller will be required to complete the deal and pay to cure the defect.

The usual solution for a defect is to convince the seller to lower the price. Often a problem appears more complicated and expensive than it really is. For example, a buyer may want to back out of a deal if he finds out that the basement leaks. But the small expense of a sump pump or a change of landscaping may solve the problem.

Other Problems

The following are some ideas for solving other problems which may come up.

•**Encroachments.** If part of the premises encroaches on the adjoining property it may be suggested that a lawsuit is necessary. But some other ways this could be solved include moving the fence, cutting the edge off the roof, cutting the edge off the driveway, or moving the garage. In many cases a minor encroachment can be overlooked by a buyer. By explaining to the seller that it would take a $5,000 lawsuit to solve the problem, and that the buyer will accept the property as is with a $2500 reduction in price, the deal may be saved and the buyer may get a better deal.

•**Termites.** In northern regions termites are not common and an infestation in a property may be reason to pass on the property. However, in warmer states most properties have some evidence of past or present infestation. Persons new to the area might be scared off by something which should be overlooked. Evidence of past treatment of the property or active termites in a fence post should not be reason to worry. The seller's clause in this book allows the seller to treat the property and force the buyer to complete the sale.

•**Judgments.** Occasionally a seller will be unaware of a judgment against himself which is a lien on the property. If it is an old one it may be difficult to find someone to release the property from the lien of the judgment. If the holder of the judgment cannot be found it may be possible to deposit the payment into the registry of the court. Once this is done it should be possible to have the title insurance policy issued. If the judgment is old enough the lien may have expired and there may be no need to pay it off.

•**Boundary Disputes.** If the survey or title report discloses a problem with the boundary of the property, it will need to be corrected whether this buyer buys the property or another does. This problem can cause a long delay, but if the owner and the affected neighbors understand the high costs of a law suit it should be possible to negotiate a compromise that can be handled with quit claim deeds.

Chapter 14
The Closing

Some of the clauses in this book may not have been seen by some closing agents before. If they have done things the same way hundreds of times they may not notice that your contract is different. Be sure to read the closing papers carefully and to compare them to the contract. Check the closing statement carefully to be sure that each item is charged to the right party.

If you have some clauses which you know are unusual you might want to call the closing agent be sure that the contract has been carefully read and is understood. This is better than having to wait for the papers to be retyped at the closing.

Some closing agents may even argue with you that "the Seller never pays for that," or that "the Buyer always pays for that in this county." Explain to them politely that none of that matters. Unless they can provide a state statute (very unlikely) or local ordinance (extremely unlikely) do not let them close except in strict compliance with your contract. In most cases, if you close under terms different from your contract you are deemed to have waived them.

It is, of course, best to have a real estate attorney attend the closing with you. That way you can be sure of your legal rights. If you have used a strong contract it may be even more important to have an attorney present. Although some attorneys insist upon charging a percentage of the purchase price, many will charge a more reasonable hourly rate or a flat fee.

In some areas where title companies handle all paperwork attorneys are rarely taken to closings. This can save a couple hundred dollars. However, the author has been to closings where the seller's deed left off part of the property (water access or several acres) which would not have been noticed by the buyer for years and would have cost thousands of dollars to correct, or may not be correctable at all. As discussed early in this book, you must weigh the cost of an attorney against your possible loss if something goes wrong.

If you decide against having an attorney attend the closing you should at least consider having the closing papers reviewed by an attorney. You can also arrange to call the attorney during the closing if problems arise.

You can specify in your contract that the closing papers will be available several days before the closing to give you and your attorney time to review them. However, some closing agents are poorly organized and do not have the papers ready until the minute of closing. In such cases they can at least be faxed to your attorney.

Whether you are the seller or the buyer you should carefully examine the closing statement, or have your attorney or broker do so. Check each figure and confirm that it has been calculated correctly. Also, check to be sure that the right party is being charged for each expense. If there are some expenses that you do not understand or which you did not request, ask that they be explained.

Unless they have been read by your attorney, you should read everything you sign. Object to anything that is incorrect or doesn't make sense. Don't swear to anything that you are not sure of. For example, title agents will often ask a buyer to sign an affidavit that there are no liens on the property. The buyer, in most cases, does not know if this is true. Before signing such a paper you should insist that the words "to the best of buyer's knowledge and belief," or "there are no liens created by buyer" are included in the affidavit.

Don't be afraid to ask questions or to object to things which do not seem right. The other people in the room will be closing agents, brokers and attorneys, and they will be professionals at what they are doing but they do make mistakes. And they are working for you and the other party. Make sure they satisfy you before you complete the deal. Don't let them rush you.

There is a rule in most states that the contract "merges with the deed" and if the closing did not follow the contract it is assumed that there was an agreement to modify the contract. In other words there is not much you can do after the closing. You cannot call back tomorrow when the attorneys are gone and say that there was a mistake made.

Buyer's Concerns

One important thing for the buyer to examine at closing is the title to the property. This is evidenced by a "title insurance binder" or, in some localities, an abstract of title. An abstract of title can usually only be examined by an experienced attorney. This is a summary of all the deeds and other papers filed in the courthouse which affect the title to the property. It usually covers every document recorded since the property first became part of the United States and can be hundreds of pages long.

A title insurance binder is a lot more readable. Typically the first section describes the property either as a lot in a subdivision or as a "metes and bounds" description. The second section describes what needs to be done to give good title to the Buyer. The third section describes the things that affect the title. This is where you find mortgages, easements and liens against the property.

The third part is also called the "exceptions" which means you have all rights to the property except those things listed. It is common to find a utility easement along the edge of the property or some subdivision restrictions which apply to the whole neighborhood and require that no businesses be conducted on the street. However, some exceptions have included easements running down the middle of the house or other things which lower the value of the property.

If you notice such a problem you definitely need the advice of an attorney. If your contract is drawn properly you can either decide to cancel the purchase or force the seller to correct the problem.

A second concern is the physical condition of the property. An inspection should have been done right before closing and if anything was not in the condition that the contract required, then an amount can be agreed upon which can be paid to the buyer to cover the problem. If the cost of solving the problem is unknown, some of the seller's funds should be held back until the problem is corrected. The title agent should have an escrow agreement available which will spell out the escrow agreement as to when the funds can be released to the seller.

Another concern of the buyer is to get physical possession of the property. Unless leases are being assumed, the buyer does not want strangers living in the property. The buyer in most cases does not want the seller to still live in the property after the closing. Either of these parties may be hard to remove.

If the seller plans to stay after closing it is also a good idea to hold some of the seller's proceeds in escrow. If the seller does not leave on time an amount can be paid to the buyer for each day the seller stays over.

Seller's Concerns

The main concern of the seller is to get paid at closing. In some states the deed and funds are placed in escrow until the funds clear. In other states the seller gets his check at the closing table.

The seller should get a cashier's check or other form of guaranteed payment and not accept a personal check from the buyer. Although the seller could sue to get the property back if the buyer's check bounced, it would be an expensive and time-consuming process. In most cases where the seller gets paid at the closing table he is paid with an escrow account check issued by the title insurance company or an attorney's trust account check. In most cases these are not a problem but in a few instances the checks have bounced when the title company went out of business after the closing. Fortunately, the underwriter of the title insurance usually made good in such cases.

To be completely safe you can insist on certified funds or a cashier's check at closing or at the close of escrow. To be sure to get this you should require it in the contract.

If the buyer will be giving the seller a mortgage or deed of trust, you should be sure that it is well-drafted and complies with the contract. If you followed this book you should have used the "Purchase Money Mortgage" and possibly the "Wraparound Mortgage" clauses.

If you will not be holding financing then you probably do not plan to have any other contact with the buyer. If problems come up such as damage to the property it is usually to agree on a figure at closing than to start an escrow and to have to deal with it later. Buyers sometimes come up with one demand after another. Old houses are expected to be in the same condition as new ones. If you can end your dealing with the buyer at the closing there is less likelihood that this will happen.

Chapter 15
After the Closing

After the closing the parties will usually not need to have further contact except in the following circumstances:

Seller Financing

If the seller is holding financing on the property the buyer will usually be making payments for many years. The relationship will end when the final payment is made and the seller releases his interest in the property, unless either party assigned their interest earlier.

If the buyer defaults in payment the seller is usually able to take the property back. This process can take considerable time and the legal fees are high. Often the seller must also continue to make payments on the first mortgage (or deed of trust) to keep that from going into foreclosure.

If the buyer finds that there are problems with the property it is tempting to stop making payments which are due to the seller. However, this is almost always a mistake since payments to the seller are not usually contingent upon the condition of the property or other factors. If problems with the seller arise the solution is usually a lawsuit, during which payments must always be kept current.

As for stopping payments to a bank or other third-party lender, don't even think of it. In most cases the lender is an even more innocent party than the buyer, and rarely subject to any liability. If you have a novel theory of lender liability that you believe applies to your case, be sure to get the opinion of an experienced real estate attorney.

Defects in the Property

As discussed in Chapter 6, there are circumstances under which a seller can be sued for defects in the property that are discovered after the sale. Such cases are usually hard to prove and both parties must usually pay their own attorney fees, so unless a large amount of money is involved, a suit is not worth the expense. If you put clauses in your contract in which the seller warranted the condition of the property, and if you used the clause stating that the contract survives the closing then you will have a much better case.

In small matters you may be able to use small claims court to sue for damages. Typically matters of up to $1,000 or $5,000 can be handled without a lawyer in small claims court.

Zoning and Building Codes

Whether a buyer can make a claim against the seller if the property is cited for violations of the zoning or building codes will depend upon the contract. If a buyer used the clauses mentioned above he will have a much better case. If the seller used the "as is" clauses, he will have the better case.

Title Problems

If you have a problem with the title to your property you will probably have recourse against the title insurance underwriter or the attorney who examined the title. Some of the types of problems that come up are, not getting all the land you were supposed to, old mortgages on the property which were not paid off and heirs or spouses of former owners who still have an interest in the property. All of these claims are serious and you should immediately contact the underwriter or attorney. If it seems that they are not handling the problem consult your own attorney.

Bills

If a buyer receives a bill for water or other services which accrued prior to the closing, it should be forwarded to the seller. If the seller does not pay it and the provider seeks to collect from the new owner the closing agent should be contacted. Some bills, such as electricity should not create liens on the property and any matters which would result in liens should be insured against by the title insurance.

Appendix
Forms

The following pages include forms which use the clauses in this book. In many cases these may be useful for a deal you are putting together. If these aren't exactly what you need you can put together your own contract using the clauses. Because these are basic contracts they may not have some of the specific clauses that you need. Be sure to read about each clause in this book and use the Addendum to Contract to add it to your contract.

The following forms are included:

> Real Estate Purchase Contract - 1 (Strong)
> Real Estate Purchase Contract - 2
> Real Estate Contract (Neutral)
> Real Estate Sales Contract - 1 (Strong)
> Real Estate Sales Contract - 2
> Addendum to Contract
> Schedule "A" (List of personal property)

REAL ESTATE PURCHASE CONTRACT - 1

Date:_____

PARTIES:_____ as
"Buyer" of_____ Phone:_____
and_____ as "Seller"
of _____ Phone:_____
hereby agree that the Buyer shall buy and the Seller shall sell real property described below under the
following terms and conditions:
Street Address:_____
Legal Description:

1. PURCHASE PRICE: The full purchase price shall be $_____ payable as follows:

   a) Deposit held in escrow by _____ $_____

   b) New mortgage* to be obtained by Buyer _____
      _____ $_____

   c) Subject to [ ] , or assumption of [ ] mortgage* to _____
      _____ with interest rate of _____%, payable $_____
      per month, having an approximate balance of...................... $_____

   d) Mortgage* and Note to be held by seller at ___% interest payable
      _____ for _____ years in the amount of.... $_____

   e) Other _____
      _____ $_____

   f) Balance to close (U.S. cash, certified or cashier's check)
      subject to adjustments and prorations, plus closing costs.... $_____

      Total .... $_____
        * or deed of trust

2. FINANCING CONTINGENCY: Contingent upon Buyer obtaining a mortgage loan for a minimum
of $_____ at a maximum interest rate of _____% with payments not to exceed $_____
per month and no more than $_____ in loan points and fees. If buyer is unable to obtain said
loan prior to closing, Buyers entire earnest money deposit shall be refunded immediately.
3. EXISTING MORTGAGES: Seller represents to Buyer that the existing mortgage on the property
is held by _____ and bears interest at _____% per
annum with monthly payments of $_____ principal and interest plus $_____ for escrow. Said
loan is fully assumable under the following terms: _____
_____ Seller to pay costs of assumption and to bring
current and transfer to Buyer the escrow balance without any additional compensation or credits. Said
balance has been calculated into the purchase price.
4. CLOSING DATE & PLACE: Closing shall be on _____, 19_____ at a location to
be selected by Buyer.
5. ACCEPTANCE: Seller shall have until _____, 19_____ at _____ o'clock ___.m. to
accept this contract.

6. PURCHASE MONEY MORTGAGES: In the event Seller will hold a purchase money mortgage under this Contract, said mortgage shall contain no prepayment penalty, be fully assumable, and allow a 60 day grace period on late payments. Mortgagee shall look only to the collateral for security and not be entitled to any deficiency judgment. Mortgagor shall have a first right of refusal at any time mortgagee desires to sell the note and mortgage at a discount, and mortgagor may have released from the mortgage, parts of the property proportional to the principal paid. Mortgagor shall be permitted to miss one monthly payment per loan year and shall be able to substitute other collateral of equal equity at any time.

7. TITLE EVIDENCE: Within _____ days from acceptance of this contract, Seller shall, at his expense, provide to Buyer a title insurance commitment for a fee simple owner's marketable title policy in the amount of the purchase price, or if it is the prevailing custom in the locality, an abstract of title, to be paid for by Seller at closing.

8. TITLE DEFECTS: In the event title is found defective, Seller shall have 60 days within which to remove such defects. If Seller is unable to cure them within such time, Buyer may cancel this contract and have all earnest money refunded or may allow Seller additional time to cure. Seller agrees to use diligent effort to correct the defects including the bringing of necessary suits.

9. EXPENSES: Seller shall pay all closing costs, documentary stamps, transfer fees and appraisals.

10. PRORATIONS: Taxes, rents, interest, property owner dues, and insurance acceptable to Buyer and _____ shall be prorated as of closing. Real and personal property taxes shall be prorated based upon the most recent available information. If closing occurs at a date when the current year's millage is not fixed, and current year's assessment is available, taxes will be prorated based upon such assessment and the prior year's millage. If current year's assessment is not available, then taxes will be prorated on the prior year's tax; provided, however, if there are improvements on the property completed by January 1st of the year of closing, which improvements were not in existence on January 1st of the prior year, then taxes shall be prorated based upon the prior year's millage and at an equitable assessment to be agreed upon between the parties, failing which, request will be made to the property appraiser or assessor for an informal assessment. Any tax proration based upon an estimate may, at the request of Buyer, be subsequently readjusted upon receipt of the tax bill. Prepaid rents and other tenant deposits shall be prorated to the date of closing.

11. SURVIVAL OF CONTRACT: This contract and the covenants herein shall survive the closing.

12. SPECIAL ASSESSMENTS: Certified, confirmed and ratified special assessment liens as of date of closing (and not as of date of Contract) are to be paid by Seller. Pending liens as of date of closing shall be assumed by Buyer, provided, however, that where the improvement has been substantially completed as of the date of closing, such pending liens shall be considered as certified, confirmed or ratified and Seller shall, at closing, be charged an amount equal to the last estimate by the public body of the assessment for the improvement.

13. LIEN AFFIDAVIT: Seller shall, as to both the real and personal property being sold hereunder, furnish to Buyer at time of closing an affidavit attesting to the absence, unless otherwise provided for herein, of any financing statements, claims of lien or potential lienors known to Seller, and further attesting that there have been no improvements to the property for 90 days immediately preceding the date of closing. If the property has been improved within said time Seller shall deliver releases or waivers of all mechanic's liens, executed by general contractors, subcontractors, suppliers and materialmen, in addition to Seller's affidavit, setting forth the names of all such parties and further reciting that in fact all bills for work to the property which could serve as a basis for a mechanic's lien have been paid or will be paid at closing.

14. CONTINGENCIES: Contingent upon the approval by Buyer's _____.

15. TERMITES: Seller, at his expense, shall provide Buyer with a report by a certified pest control operator acceptable to Buyer, dated within 30 days of closing, that there are no signs of infestation by wood destroying organisms. In the event infestation is indicated, Buyer may cancel this contract, or

the property shall be treated and repaired at the expense of Seller.

16. SURVEY: Seller shall provide Buyer with a survey of the property certified within 30 days of closing. In the event encroachments are indicated they shall be corrected at the expense of Seller.

17. LEASES: Contingent upon Buyer's approval of all leases affecting the property, copies of which shall be provided to buyer five days after acceptance hereof. Prior to closing, Seller shall furnish to Buyer estoppel letters from all tenants stating the nature and duration of occupancy, rental terms and advanced rent and security deposits. In the event Seller is unable to obtain such letters, said information shall be furnished by Seller to Buyer in the form of a Seller's affidavit and Buyer may thereafter contact tenants to confirm such information. Seller shall deliver and assign to Buyer all original leases at closing along with an assignment of all leases.

18. PERSONAL PROPERTY: This sale includes all items of personal property listed on Schedule "A" to be attached hereto plus all additional items remaining on the premises after closing. Seller warrants all items to be in working order at time of closing.

19. ALLOCATION OF PURCHASE PRICE: The parties agree that the allocation of the purchase price is $_____ for the land, $_____ for the buildings, and $_____ for the personal property. The parties agree that the sale is indivisible even though the amounts have been allocated separately.

20. MAINTENANCE: Seller agrees to deliver the premises in good condition. Until the closing the Seller shall maintain the property, including the lawn and shrubbery, and the pool, if any, shall be clean and clear. All floors to be washed or vacuumed and all walls to be clean and free of holes or damage. The lawn and shrubbery shall be maintained and the pool, if any, shall be clean and clear. All floors to be washed or vacuumed and all walls to be clean and free of holes or damage.

21. INSPECTION: Buyer shall be allowed to inspect the property within 24 hours of closing and at such time Seller shall have the electrical service and water and gas on.

22. PLUMBING AND ELECTRICAL: Seller warrants all heating, cooling, electrical and plumbing systems to be in working condition as of closing. Buyer may have inspections made of said systems by licensed persons dealing in the repair and maintenance thereof. All plumbing to be free from drips or leaks and in conformance with applicable standards, including septic system, if any, and all electrical fixtures to be in working order including bulbs.

23. RESTRICTIONS & EASEMENTS: Sale contingent upon property being free and clear of any easements or restrictions which adversely affect the value of the property to Buyer. Seller to provide copies thereof at least 15 days prior to closing.

24. CONDOMINIUMS - 1: If this property is a condominium Buyer shall be given a copy of the Declaration of Condominium and all Amendments and rules and regulations promulgated thereunder within five days of acceptance of this Contract. Buyer shall have the option to cancel this contract if said documents are not satisfactory to his needs.

25. CONDOMINIUMS - 2: If this property is a condominium, Seller shall convey all rights therein including common elements and limited common elements such as parking spaces and cabanas, if any. This Contract is contingent upon approval by the association or developer, if required, and Seller shall pay all costs of approval and transfer. Any assessments to be levied for work, improvements or services, which are substantially completed at time of closing, shall be paid by Seller.

26. ZONING & ORDINANCES: Contingent upon zoning and ordinances not affecting Buyer's intended use of the property.

27. ROOF: The Seller, within the time allowed for delivery of evidence of title and examination thereof, or no later than ten days prior to closing, whichever date occurs last, shall have the roof inspected at Seller's expense by a licensed roofer, licensed general contractor or a firm specializing in presale inspections of property to determine that there is no visible evidence of leaks or damage (including facia and soffit.) If repairs are needed, Seller shall have them completed at his expense by a licensed roofer, or at Buyer's option shall credit the Buyer for the cost of said repairs.

28. VIOLATIONS: Seller warrants property to be free from violations of building, health and other governmental codes and ordinances.

29. Seller warrants that the property is not in violation of any federal, state or local environmental laws.

30. INGRESS & EGRESS: Seller warrants that there is ingress and egress to the property which is insurable by a title insurance underwriter.

31. ASSIGNMENT: Buyer may assign this contract and all rights and obligations hereunder to another person, corporation or trustee.

32. POSSESSION: Seller shall deliver exclusive possession of the premises to Buyer at closing subject only to leases assigned to buyer which are current in rent. In the event any rents are in arrears, the sum of $500.00 of Seller's funds shall be held in escrow by closing agent for each unit in arrears, to cover the costs of eviction and lost rent, if any. If Seller is to remain in possession of the property at closing, Seller's proceeds shall not be released until Seller has fully vacated the property, and Buyer shall be entitled to $50.00 per day for each day Seller holds over.

33. RISK OF LOSS: If the improvements are damaged by fire or other casualty prior to closing, Buyer shall have the option of either taking the property as is together with the insurance proceeds available by virtue of such loss or damage, or of cancelling this contract and receiving return of deposits made hereunder.

34. DEFAULT: In the event Buyer defaults hereunder, Seller shall be entitled to the earnest money deposited herewith as liquidated damages. In the event Seller defaults hereunder, Buyer may proceed at law or in equity to enforce his rights under this contract.

35. ATTORNEY'S FEES: In the event Seller breaches this Contract, Buyer shall be entitled to recover reasonable attorney's fees and costs.

36. CONVEYANCE: Conveyance shall be by Warranty Deed subject only to matters excepted in this contract. Personal property shall be conveyed by an absolute Bill of Sale with warranty of title subject only to such liens as provided herein.

37. SEVERABILITY: In the event any clause in this contract is held to be unenforceable, or against public policy, such holding shall not affect the validity of the remainder of the contract unless it materially alters the terms hereof.

38. OTHER AGREEMENTS: No prior or present agreements or representations shall be binding upon the parties unless incorporated into this contract. No modification or change in this contract shall be binding unless in writing and signed by the party to be bound thereby.

Having read the foregoing, the undersigned hereby ratify, approve and confirm the same as our agreement.

Witnesses: Sellers:

_____   _____

_____   _____

                                                     Buyers:

_____   _____

_____   _____

110

REAL ESTATE PURCHASE CONTRACT - 2

Date:_____

PARTIES:_____ as

"Buyer" of_____ Phone:_____

and_____ as "Seller"

of _____ Phone:_____

hereby agree that the Buyer shall buy and the Seller shall sell real property described below under the following terms and conditions:

Street Address:_____

Legal Description:

1. PURCHASE PRICE: The full purchase price shall be $_____ payable as follows:

    a) Deposit held in escrow by _____ $_____

    b) New mortgage* to be obtained by Buyer _____

         _____ $_____

    c) Subject to [ ] , or assumption of [ ] mortgage* to _____

         _____ with interest rate of _____%, payable $_____

         per month, having an approximate balance of...................... $_____

    d) Mortgage* and Note to be held by seller at ___% interest payable

         _____ for _____ years in the amount of.... $_____

    e) Other _____

         _____ $_____

    f) Balance to close (U.S. cash, certified or cashier's check)

         subject to adjustments and prorations, plus closing costs.... $_____

         Total .... $_____
           * or deed of trust

2. FINANCING CONTINGENCY: Contingent upon Buyer obtaining a mortgage loan for a minimum of $_____ at a maximum interest rate of _____% with payments not to exceed $_____ per month and no more than $_____ in loan points and fees.

3. EXISTING MORTGAGES: Seller represents to Buyer that the existing mortgage on the property is held by _____ and bears interest at _____% per annum with monthly payments of $_____ principal and interest plus $_____ for escrow. Said loan is fully assumable under the following terms: _____

_____ .

4. CLOSING DATE & PLACE: Closing shall be on _____, 19_____ at a location to be selected by Buyer.

5. ACCEPTANCE: Seller shall have until _____, 19_____ at _____ o'clock ___.m. to accept this contract.

6. PURCHASE MONEY MORTGAGES: In the event Seller will hold a purchase money mortgage under this Contract, said mortgage shall contain no prepayment penalty, be fully assumable, and allow a 30 day grace period on late payments. Mortgagee shall look only to the collateral for security and

not be entitled to any deficiency judgment. Mortgagor shall have a first right of refusal at any time mortgagee desires to sell the note and mortgage at a discount.

7. TITLE EVIDENCE: Within _____ days from acceptance of this contract, Seller shall, at his expense, provide to Buyer a title insurance commitment for a fee simple owner's marketable title policy in the amount of the purchase price, or if it is the prevailing custom in the locality, an abstract of title, to be paid for by Seller at closing.

8. TITLE DEFECTS: In the event title is found defective, Seller shall have 60 days within which to remove such defects. If Seller is unable to cure them within such time, Buyer may cancel this contract and have all earnest money refunded or may allow Seller additional time to cure. Seller agrees to use diligent effort to correct the defects including the bringing of necessary suits.

9. EXPENSES: Seller shall pay for the documentary stamps or transfer taxes on the deed, costs of obtaining and recording any corrective instruments and for any intangible taxes and recording of any mortgages to be executed by Buyer.

10. PRORATIONS: Taxes, rents, interest, property owner dues, and insurance acceptable to Buyer and _____ shall be prorated as of closing. Real and personal property taxes shall be prorated based upon the most recent available information. If closing occurs at a date when the current year's millage is not fixed, and current year's assessment is available, taxes will be prorated based upon such assessment and the prior year's millage. If current year's assessment is not available, then taxes will be prorated on the prior year's tax; provided, however, if there are improvements on the property completed by January 1st of the year of closing, which improvements were not in existence on January 1st of the prior year, then taxes shall be prorated based upon the prior year's millage and at an equitable assessment to be agreed upon between the parties, failing which, request will be made to the property appraiser or assessor for an informal assessment. Any tax proration based upon an estimate may, at the request of Buyer, be subsequently readjusted upon receipt of the tax bill. Prepaid rents and other tenant deposits shall be prorated to the date of closing. Any security deposits shall be turned over to Buyer.

11. SURVIVAL OF CONTRACT: This contract and the covenants herein shall survive the closing.

12. SPECIAL ASSESSMENTS: Certified, confirmed and ratified special assessment liens as of date of closing (and not as of date of Contract) are to be paid by Seller. Pending liens as of date of closing shall be assumed by Buyer.

13. LIEN AFFIDAVIT: Seller shall, as to both the real and personal property being sold hereunder, furnish to Buyer at time of closing an affidavit attesting to the absence, unless otherwise provided for herein, of any financing statements, claims of lien or potential lienors known to Seller, and further attesting that there have been no improvements to the property for 90 days immediately preceding the date of closing. If the property has been improved within said time Seller shall deliver releases or waivers of all mechanic's liens, executed by general contractors, subcontractors, suppliers and materialmen, in addition to Seller's affidavit, setting forth the names of all such parties and further reciting that in fact all bills for work to the property which could serve as a basis for a mechanic's lien have been paid or will be paid at closing.

14. CONTINGENCIES: Contingent upon the approval by Buyer's _____.

15. TERMITES: Seller, at his expense, shall provide Buyer with a report by a certified pest control operator acceptable to Buyer, dated within 30 days of closing, that there are no signs of infestation by wood destroying organisms. In the event infestation is indicated, Buyer may cancel this contract, or the property shall be treated and repaired at the expense of Seller of up to 3% of the purchase price.

16. SURVEY: Seller shall provide Buyer with a survey of the property certified within 30 days of closing. In the event encroachments are indicated they shall be corrected at the expense of Seller.

17. LEASES: Contingent upon Buyer's approval of all leases affecting the property, copies of which shall be provided to buyer five days after acceptance hereof. Prior to closing, Seller shall furnish to Buyer estoppel letters from all tenants stating the nature and duration of occupancy, rental terms and

advanced rent and security deposits. In the event Seller is unable to obtain such letters, said information shall be furnished by Seller to Buyer in the form of a Seller's affidavit and Buyer may thereafter contact tenants to confirm such information. Seller shall deliver and assign to Buyer all original leases at closing along with an assignment of all leases.

18. PERSONAL PROPERTY: This sale includes all items of personal property listed on Schedule "A" to be attached hereto plus all additional items remaining on the premises after closing. Seller warrants all items to be in working order at time of closing.

19. ALLOCATION OF PURCHASE PRICE: The parties agree that the allocation of the purchase price is $_____ for the land, $_____ for the buildings, and $_____ for the personal property. The parties agree that the sale is indivisible even though the amounts have been allocated separately.

20. MAINTENANCE: Seller agrees to deliver the premises in good condition. Until the closing the Seller shall maintain the property, including the lawn and shrubbery, and the pool, if any, shall be clean and clear. All floors to be washed or vacuumed and all walls to be clean and free of holes or damage. The lawn and shrubbery shall be maintained and the pool, if any, shall be clean and clear. All floors to be washed or vacuumed and all walls to be clean and free of holes or damage.

21. INSPECTION: Buyer shall be allowed to inspect the property within 24 hours of closing and at such time Seller shall have the electrical service and water and gas on.

22. PLUMBING AND ELECTRICAL: Seller warrants all heating, cooling, electrical and plumbing systems to be in working condition as of closing.

23. RESTRICTIONS & EASEMENTS: Sale contingent upon property being free and clear of any easements or restrictions which adversely affect the value of the property to Buyer.

24. CONDOMINIUMS - 1: If this property is a condominium, sale is contingent upon Buyer's attorney approving the Declaration of Condominium and all Amendments thereto and any rules and regulations promulgated thereunder.

25. CONDOMINIUMS - 2: If this property is a condominium, Seller shall convey all rights therein including common elements and limited common elements such as parking spaces and cabanas, if any. This Contract is contingent upon approval by the association or developer, if required, and Seller shall pay all costs of approval and transfer. Any assessments to be levied for work, improvements or services, which are substantially completed at time of closing, shall be paid by Seller.

26. ZONING & ORDINANCES: Contingent upon zoning and ordinances not affecting Buyer's intended use of the property.

27. ROOF: The Seller, within the time allowed for delivery of evidence of title and examination thereof, or no later than ten days prior to closing, whichever date occurs last, shall have the roof inspected at Seller's expense by a licensed roofer, licensed general contractor or a firm specializing in presale inspections of property to determine that there is no visible evidence of leaks or damage (including facia and soffit.) If repairs are needed, Seller shall have them completed at his expense by a licensed roofer, or at Buyer's option shall credit the Buyer for the cost of said repairs.

28. VIOLATIONS: Seller warrants property to be free from violations of building, health and other governmental codes and ordinances.

29. Seller warrants that the property is not in violation of any federal, state or local environmental laws.

30. INGRESS & EGRESS: Seller warrants that there is ingress and egress to the property which is insurable by a title insurance underwriter.

31. ASSIGNMENT: This contract is fully assignable.

32. POSSESSION: Seller shall deliver exclusive possession of the premises to Buyer at closing subject only to leases assigned to buyer which are current in rent.

33. RISK OF LOSS: If the improvements are damaged by fire or other casualty prior to closing, Buyer shall have the option of either taking the property as is together with the insurance proceeds available by virtue of such loss or damage, or of cancelling this contract and receiving return of deposits made

hereunder.

34. DEFAULT: In the event Buyer defaults hereunder, Seller shall be entitled to the earnest money deposited herewith as liquidated damages. In the event Seller defaults hereunder, Buyer may proceed at law or in equity to enforce his rights under this contract.

35. ATTORNEYS' FEES: In connection with any litigation, including appellate proceedings, arising out of this Contract, the prevailing party shall be entitled to recover attorneys' fees and costs.

36. CONVEYANCE: Conveyance shall be by Warranty Deed subject only to matters excepted in this contract. Personal property shall be conveyed by absolute Bill of Sale with warranty of title subject only to such liens as provided herein.

37. SEVERABILITY: In the event any clause in this contract is held to be unenforceable, or against public policy, such holding shall not affect the validity of the remainder of the contract unless it materially alters the terms hereof.

38. OTHER AGREEMENTS: No prior or present agreements or representations shall be binding upon the parties unless incorporated into this contract. No modification or change in this contract shall be binding unless in writing and signed by the party to be bound thereby.

Having read the foregoing, the undersigned hereby ratify, approve and confirm the same as our agreement.

Witnesses: Sellers:

_____   _____

_____   _____

                                              Buyers:

_____   _____

_____   _____

REAL ESTATE CONTRACT

Date:_____

PARTIES:_____ as
"Buyer" of_____ Phone:_____
and_____ as "Seller"
of _____ Phone:_____
hereby agree that the Buyer shall buy and the Seller shall sell real property described below under the following terms and conditions:
Street Address:_____
Legal Description:

1. PURCHASE PRICE: The full purchase price shall be $_____ payable as follows:

   a) Deposit held in escrow by _____ $_____

   b) New mortgage* to be obtained by Buyer _____
      _____ $_____

   c) Subject to [ ] , or assumption of [ ] mortgage* to _____
      _____ with interest rate of _____%, payable $_____
      per month, having an approximate balance of....................... $_____

   d) Mortgage* and Note to be held by seller at ___% interest payable
      _____ for _____ years in the amount of.... $_____

   e) Other _____
      _____ $_____

   f) Balance to close (U.S. cash, certified or cashier's check)
      subject to adjustments and prorations, plus closing costs.... $_____

     Total .... $_____
              * or deed of trust

1. FINANCING: Contingent upon Buyer obtaining a firm commitment for a mortgage loan for a minimum of $_____ at a maximum interest rate of _____% for a term of at least ____years. Buyer agrees to make application for and use reasonable diligence to obtain said loan.

2. EXISTING MORTGAGES: Seller represents to Buyer that the existing mortgage on the property is held by _____ and bears interest at _____% per annum with monthly payments of $_____ principal and interest plus $_____ for escrow. Said loan is fully assumable under the following terms: _____

3. CLOSING DATE & PLACE: Closing shall be on _____, 19_____ at the office of the attorney or title agent selected by Seller.

4. ACCEPTANCE: If this contract is not executed by both parties on or before _____, 19_____ it shall be void and Buyer's deposit returned.

5. PERSONAL PROPERTY: This sale includes all personal property listed on Schedule A. The parties agree that the portion of the purchase price attributable to these items is $_____.

6. TITLE EVIDENCE: Seller shall purchase and deliver to Buyer at or before closing a title insurance policy, or if it is the prevailing custom in the locality, an abstract of title.

7. TITLE DEFECTS: In the event title is found defective, Seller shall have 60 days within which to remove such defects. If Seller is unable to cure them within such time, Buyer may cancel this contract and have all earnest money refunded or may allow Seller additional time to cure. Seller agrees to use diligent effort to correct the defects including the bringing of necessary suits.

8. PRORATIONS: Real and personal property taxes shall be prorated based upon the most recent available information. If closing occurs at a date when the current year's millage is not fixed, and the current year's assessment is available, taxes will be prorated based upon such assessment and the prior year's millage. If current year's assessment is not available, then taxes will be prorated on the prior year's tax; provided, however, that if there are improvements on the property completed by January 1st of the year of closing, which were not in existence on January 1st of the prior year, then taxes shall be prorated based upon the prior year's millage and at an equitable assessment to be agreed upon between the parties, failing which, request will be made to the County Property Appraiser for an informal assessment. Any tax proration based upon an estimate may, at the request of either party, be subsequently readjusted upon receipt of the tax bill. Prepaid rents and other tenant deposits shall be prorated to the date of closing.

9. EXPENSES: The parties herein shall each pay half of the costs and fees for closing costs, documentary stamps and transfer and recording fees.

10. SPECIAL ASSESSMENTS: Certified, confirmed and ratified special assessment liens as of date of closing (and not as of closing date) are to be paid by Seller. Pending liens as of date of closing shall be assumed by Buyer.

11. LIEN AFFIDAVIT: Seller shall, as to both the real and personal property being sold hereunder, furnish to Buyer at time of closing an affidavit attesting to the absence, unless otherwise provided for herein, of any financing statements, claims of lien or potential lienors known to Seller, and further attesting that there have been no improvements to the property for 90 days immediately preceding the date of closing. If the property has been improved within said time Seller shall deliver releases or waivers of all mechanic's liens, executed by general contractors, subcontractors, suppliers and materialmen, in addition to Seller's affidavit, setting forth the names of all such parties and further reciting that in fact all bills for work to the property which could serve as a basis for a mechanic's lien have been paid or will be paid at closing.

12. CONTINGENCIES: Contingent upon satisfactory inspection of the premises by a licensed contractor.

13. TERMITES: Within 30 days of closing the premises shall be inspected by a certified pest control operator acceptable to Buyer and the cost of said inspection shall be paid equally by Buyer and Seller. In the event infestation by wood destroying organisms is indicated, either party may cancel this contract or Seller may treat the premises at his expense if acceptable to Buyer.

14. PLUMBING AND ELECTRICAL: Major appliances, heating, cooling, electrical and plumbing systems to be in working order as of 6 days prior to closing. Buyer may inspect said items and shall report in writing to seller such items as found not to be in working condition. Unless Buyer reports failures by said date he shall be deemed to have waived Seller's warranty as to failures not reported. Valid reported failures shall be corrected at Seller's cost. Seller agrees to provide access for inspection upon reasonable notice.

15. RESTRICTIONS & EASEMENTS: Property is subject to easements, covenants and restrictions of record provided they do not affect Buyer's intended use of the property.

16. CONDOMINIUMS - 1: If this property is a condominium, sale is contingent upon Buyer or his attorney approving the Declaration of Condominium and all Amendments thereto and any rules and regulations promulgated thereunder within 15 days of receipt from Seller.

17. CONDOMINIUMS - 2: If this property is a condominium, Seller shall convey all rights therein including common elements such as parking spaces and cabanas, if any. This contract is contingent upon the approval by the association or developer, if required, and the parties shall equally pay all costs of approval and transfer. Any assessments shall be prorated as of closing.

18. ZONING & ORDINANCES: Property is subject to governmental zoning and ordinances. VIOLATIONS: Seller represents that he has received no notice of violation on the property of any building, health or other governmental codes or ordinances.

19. INGRESS & EGRESS: Seller warrants that there is ingress and egress to the property which is insurable by a title insurance underwriter.

20. POSSESSION: Seller shall deliver exclusive possession of the premises to Buyer at closing subject only to leases assigned to Buyer.

21. RISK OF LOSS: If the improvements are damaged by fire or other casualty prior to closing, and the cost of restoring same does not exceed 3% of the assessed valuation of the improvements so damaged, Buyer shall have the option of either taking the property as is together with either the 3% or any insurance proceeds available by virtue of such loss or damage, or of cancelling this contract and receiving return of deposits made hereunder.

22. DEFAULT: If the Buyer fails to perform under this contract within the time specified, the deposit(s) paid by the Buyer may be retained by the Seller as liquidated damages, consideration for the execution of this contract and full settlement of any claims, whereupon all parties shall be relieved of all obligations under this contract. If, for any reason other than failure of Seller to render his title marketable after diligent effort, Seller fails, neglects, or refuses to perform under this contract, Buyer may proceed at law or in equity to enforce his rights under this contract.

23. ARBITRATION: In the event of any dispute under this contract the parties agree to binding arbitration under the rules of the American Arbitration Association.

24. CONVEYANCE: Conveyance shall be by Warranty Deed subject only to matters excepted in this contract. Personal property shall, at the request of Buyer be conveyed by an absolute Bill of Sale with warranty of title subject only to such liens as provided herein.

25. SEVERABILITY: In the event any clause in this contract is held to be unenforceable, or against public policy, such holding shall not affect the validity of the remainder of the contract unless it materially alters the terms hereof.

26. OTHER AGREEMENTS: No prior or present agreements or representations shall be binding upon the parties unless incorporated into this contract. No modification or change in this contract shall be binding unless in writing and signed by the party to be bound thereby.

Having read the foregoing, the undersigned hereby ratify, approve and confirm the same as our agreement.

Witnesses:

_____

_____

Sellers:

_____

_____

Buyers:

_____

_____

REAL ESTATE SALES CONTRACT -1

Date:_____

PARTIES:_____ as

"Buyer" of_____ Phone:_____

and_____ as "Seller"

of _____ Phone:_____

hereby agree that the Buyer shall buy and the Seller shall sell real property described below under the following terms and conditions:

Street Address:_____

Legal Description:

1. PURCHASE PRICE: The full purchase price shall be $_____ payable as follows:

   a) Deposit held in escrow by _____ $_____

   b) New mortgage* to be obtained by Buyer _____

       _____ $_____

   c) Subject to [ ] , or assumption of [ ] mortgage* to _____
       _____ with interest rate of _____%, payable $_____
       per month, having an approximate balance of...................... $_____

   d) Mortgage* and Note to be held by seller at ___% interest payable
       _____ for _____ years in the amount of.... $_____

   e) Other _____
       _____ $_____

   f) Balance to close (U.S. cash, certified or cashier's check)
       subject to adjustments and prorations, plus closing costs.... $_____

       Total .... $_____
       * or deed of trust

2. EXISTING MORTGAGES: Buyer to assume and hold Seller harmless on mortgage to _____. Buyer to pay all costs of assumption and to purchase Seller's escrow balance, if any.

3. CLOSING DATE & PLACE: Closing shall be on _____, 19_____ at a location to be selected by Seller. Time is of the essence.

4. PURCHASE MONEY MORTGAGES: In the event Seller will hold a mortgage under this contract, said mortgage will be on a standard form used by lenders in the area and contain a "due on sale clause."

5. ACCEPTANCE: Buyer shall have until _____, 19____ at ___ o'clock __.m. in which to accept this contract.

6. PERSONAL PROPERTY: The following personal property is included in the purchase price and is sold in "as is" condition: _____.

7. TITLE EVIDENCE: Buyer may, at his expense, obtain a title insurance policy or abstract of title.

8. TITLE DEFECTS: In the event title is found defective, Buyer shall within three days thereafter notify Seller in writing specifying the defects or else same shall be waived. If defects render title unmarketable, Seller shall have 180 days within which to cure said defects or to cancel this contract.

9. EXPENSES: Buyer shall pay all closing costs, including documentary stamps and transfer fees.

10. PRORATIONS: Neither taxes nor rents shall be prorated as these have been calculated into the sales price.

11. LEASES: Property to be conveyed subject to existing leases and tenancies, if any.

12. INSPECTION: Property is being sold in "as is" condition with no representations or warranties of any nature being given by seller. Buyer has personally fully inspected the property, finds it satisfactory and does not rely on any representations not contained in this contract.

13. ZONING & ORDINANCES: Property to be conveyed subject to governmental zoning and ordinances.

14. RECORDING: Neither this contract nor any notice of it shall be recorded in any public records.

15. CONDOMINIUMS: If this property is a condominium requiring approval by the association or developer, Buyer shall make application within five days of acceptance of this contract and shall pay all approval and transfer fees, if any. Any assessments shall be prorated as of closing.

16. ASSIGNMENT: This contract is personal to the parties and is not assignable.

17. POSSESSION: Possession shall be delivered at closing subject to existing tenancies, if any.

18. RISK OF LOSS: If the improvements are damaged by fire or other casualty prior to closing, Seller may cancel this Contract, or may extend the closing date up to 90 days and restore them to substantially their original condition.

19. DEFAULT: In the event Buyer defaults hereunder, Seller shall be entitled to retain any deposits paid hereunder as liquidated damages, or at his option, Seller may proceed to enforce specific performance of this contract. In the event Seller defaults hereunder, Buyer shall be entitled to the sum $_____ as liquidated damages from the Seller plus return of Buyer's deposit, if any.

20. ATTORNEY'S FEES: In the event Buyer breaches this Contract, Seller shall be entitled to recover reasonable attorney's fees and costs.

21. CONVEYANCE: Conveyance shall be by Fee Simple Deed

22. SEVERABILITY: In the event any clause in this contract is held to be unenforceable or against public policy, such holding shall not affect the validity of the remainder of the contract unless it materially alters the terms hereof.

23. OTHER AGREEMENTS: No prior or present agreements or representations shall be binding upon the parties unless incorporated into this contract. No modification or change in this contract shall be binding unless in writing and signed by the party to be bound thereby.

Having read the foregoing, the undersigned hereby ratify, approve and confirm the same as our agreement.

Witnesses: Sellers:

_____   _____

_____   _____

                                                    Buyers:

_____   _____

_____   _____

REAL ESTATE SALES CONTRACT -2

Date:_____

PARTIES:_____ as
"Buyer" of_____ Phone:_____
and_____ as "Seller"
of _____ Phone:_____
hereby agree that the Buyer shall buy and the Seller shall sell real property described below under the following terms and conditions:

Street Address:_____

Legal Description:

1. PURCHASE PRICE: The full purchase price shall be $_____ payable as follows:

   a) Deposit held in escrow by _____ $_____

   b) New mortgage* to be obtained by Buyer _____
       _____ $_____

   c) Subject to [ ] , or assumption of [ ] mortgage* to _____
       _____ with interest rate of _____%, payable $_____
       per month, having an approximate balance of....................... $_____

   d) Mortgage* and Note to be held by seller at ___% interest payable
       _____ for _____ years in the amount of.... $_____

   e) Other _____
       _____ $_____

   f) Balance to close (U.S. cash, certified or cashier's check)
       subject to adjustments and prorations, plus closing costs.... $_____

       Total .... $_____
       * or deed of trust

2. EXISTING MORTGAGES: Buyer to assume and hold Seller harmless on mortgage to
_____.

3. CLOSING DATE & PLACE: Closing shall be on _____, 19_____ at a location to be selected by Seller. Time is of the essence.

4. PURCHASE MONEY MORTGAGES: In the event Seller will hold a mortgage under this contract, said mortgage will be on a standard form used by lenders in the area and contain a "due on sale clause."

5. ACCEPTANCE: Buyer shall have until _____, 19____ at ___ o'clock ___.m. in which to accept this contract.

6. PERSONAL PROPERTY: The following personal property is included in the purchase price and is sold in "as is" condition: _____.

7. TITLE EVIDENCE: Buyer may, at his expense, obtain a title insurance policy or abstract of title.

8. TITLE DEFECTS: In the event title is found defective, Buyer shall within three days thereafter notify Seller in writing specifying the defects or else same shall be waived. If defects render title unmarketable, Seller shall have 120 days within which to cure said defects or to cancel this contract.

9. EXPENSES: Buyer shall pay all closing costs, including documentary stamps and transfer fees.

10. PRORATIONS: Real and personal property taxes shall be prorated according to the last available bill and no future adjustments required. Rents and other tenant deposits shall be prorated as the date of closing.

11. LEASES: Property to be conveyed subject to existing leases and tenancies, if any.

12. INSPECTION: Property is being sold in "as is" condition with no representations or warranties of any nature being given by seller. Buyer has personally fully inspected the property, finds it satisfactory and does not rely on any representations not contained in this contract.

13. ZONING & ORDINANCES: Property to be conveyed subject to governmental zoning and ordinances.

14. RECORDING: Neither this contract nor any notice of it shall be recorded in any public records.

15. CONDOMINIUMS: If this property is a condominium requiring approval by the association or developer, Buyer shall make application within five days of acceptance of this contract and shall pay all approval and transfer fees, if any. Any assessments shall be prorated as of closing.

16. ASSIGNMENT: This contract is not assignable.

17. POSSESSION: Possession shall be delivered at closing subject to existing tenancies, if any.

18. RISK OF LOSS: If the improvements are damaged by fire or other casualty prior to closing, Seller may cancel this Contract, or may extend the closing date up to 90 days and restore them to substantially their original condition.

19. DEFAULT: In the event Buyer defaults hereunder, Seller shall be entitled to retain any deposits paid hereunder as liquidated damages, or at his option, Seller may proceed to enforce specific performance of this contract. In the event Seller defaults hereunder, Buyer shall be entitled to the sum $_____ as liquidated damages from the Seller plus return of Buyer's deposit, if any.

20. ATTORNEY'S FEES: In connection with any litigation, including appellate proceedings, arising out of this contract, the prevailing party shall be entitled to recover reasonable attorney's fees and costs.

21. CONVEYANCE: Conveyance shall be by Fee Simple Deed

22. SEVERABILITY: In the event any clause in this contract is held to be unenforceable or against public policy, such holding shall not affect the validity of the remainder of the contract unless it materially alters the terms hereof.

23. OTHER AGREEMENTS: No prior or present agreements or representations shall be binding upon the parties unless incorporated into this contract. No modification or change in this contract shall be binding unless in writing and signed by the party to be bound thereby.

Having read the foregoing, the undersigned hereby ratify, approve and confirm the same as our agreement.

Witnesses: Sellers:

_____   _____

_____   _____

                                                          Buyers:

_____   _____

_____   _____

ADDENDUM

The undersigned parties to that certain Real Estate Contract on _____

_____ dated _____, 19____,

hereby agree that the following terms are hereby made a part of that contract and supersede any terms

to the contrary in said contract.

Having read the foregoing, the undersigned hereby ratify, approve and confirm the same as our agreement.

Witnesses: Sellers:

_____   _____

_____   _____

                                               Buyers:

_____   _____

_____   _____

SCHEDULE A

The following personal property is included in the sale of _____
_____ (List quantities, make and condition)

_____	Range	_____
_____	Oven	_____
_____	Refrigerator	_____
_____	Freezer	_____
_____	Dishwasher	_____
_____	Disposal	_____
_____	Microwave	_____
_____	Washer	_____
_____	Dryer	_____
_____	Heating System	_____
_____	Air System	_____
_____	Air Units	_____
_____	Mowers	_____
_____	Water Heater	_____
_____	Water Softener	_____
_____	Dehumidifier	_____
_____	Ceiling Fans	_____
_____	Pool Equipment	_____
_____	Fireplace Equipment	_____
_____	Swing Set	_____
_____	Barbecue	_____
_____	Rods	_____
_____	Blinds	_____
_____	Rugs	_____
_____	Shades	_____
_____	Curtains & Drapes	_____
_____	Lawn Equipment	_____
_____	Other	_____
_____	Other	_____
_____	Other	_____
_____	Other	_____
_____	Other	_____
_____	Other	_____
_____	Other	_____

Unless otherwise specified the property included with this sale is the same property viewed by Buyer when the property was examined.

Initials of the parties: _____ _____ _____ _____

Index

Sphinx Publishing Presents

Self-Help Law Books

Laymen's Guides to The Law

What our customers say about our books:

"It couldn't be more clear for the lay person." R.D.

"I want you to know I really appreciate your book. It has saved me a lot of time and money." L.T.

"Your real estate contracts book has saved me nearly $12,000.00 in closing costs over the past year." A.B.

"...many of the legal questions that I have had over the years were answered clearly and concisely through your plain English interpretation of the law." C.E.H.

"If there weren't people out there like you I'd be lost. You have the best books of this type out there." S.B.

"...your forms and directions are easy to follow..." C.V.M.

Sphinx titles are available directly from the publisher or from independent book stores and chain stores such as B. Dalton, Bookland, Bookstop, and Waldenbooks.

Our National titles are valid in all 50 States

Popular Legal Topics

- **How to File Your Own Bankruptcy** (or How to Avoid It) By Edward Haman, Atty., 2nd Ed., $19.95
  Explains how to evaluate your financial situation, consider the options and file your own bankruptcy, if necessary.

- **Debtors' Rights, A Legal Self-Help Guide** By Gudrun Nickel, Atty., $12.95
  Explains the legal rights of people who owe money in all types of matters.

- **Neighbor vs. Neighbor**, Legal Rights of Neighbors in Dispute By Mark Warda, Atty., $12.95
  Explains all the laws and legal principles involved in neighbor disputes. Includes over 400 true cases.

- **How to Register a United States Copyright** By Mark Warda, Atty., 3rd Ed., $14.95
  Explains what a copyright is, what can and cannot be copyrighted, benefits of registration and more.

- **How to Register a United States Trademark** By Mark Warda, Atty., 3rd Ed., $14.95
  Explains benefits of registration, searching and choosing a trademark, and the types of registration.

- **U. S. A. Immigration Guide** By Ramon Carrion, Atty., $19.95.
  Explains the immigration process including new opportunities for Green Cards & Visas.

  "Filers must pay a $120.00 court fee, but there's no legal requirements to have an attorney. Rather, do-it-yourselfers can turn to books, such as $19.95 paperback How to File Your Own Bankruptcy (or How to Avoid It) from Sphinx Publishing in Clearwater, Fl."
  Business Week

> **How to File Your Own Bankruptcy** (or How to Avoid It)
>
> With Forms
>
> Includes
> Chapter 7 (Discharge of Debts)
> Chapter 13 (Payment Plan)
>
> Sphinx Publishing

- **How to File Your Own Divorce** By Edward Haman, Atty., $19.95
  Explains all aspects of filing for a divorce, including alimony and child support. Includes laws of all 50 states.

- **How to Form Your Own Corporation** By Kelsea Wilber & Arthur Sartorious, Attys., $19.95
  Explains how to register a for profit corporation, including corporate minutes.

- **How to Write Your Own Premarital Agreement** By Edward Haman, Atty., $19.95
  Provides instructions and forms for writing a premarital agreement

- **How to Write Your Own Partnership Agreement** By Edward Haman, Atty., $19.95
  Explains how to write a sound partnership agreement.

- **The Power of Attorney Handbook** By Edward Haman, Atty., $19.95
  Explains an official way to give someone else authorization to handle particular transactions for specific amounts of time.

- **How to Negotiate Real Estate Contracts** By Mark Warda, Atty., $14.95
  Explains in simple language the type of clauses used and why different versions are better for buyers or sellers.

- **How to Negotiate Real Estate Leases** By Mark Warda, Atty., $14.95
  Explains in simple language each clause used in leases and which version is best for land lords or tenants.

"Debtors' Rights . . . a very good reference and source of information for debtor decision-making."
George Hampton, Booklist

Our Florida titles cover most areas of the law

Family and Personal Matters

- **How to Make a Florida Will** By Mark Warda, Atty., 3rd Ed., $9.95
  Explains in simple language who can make a Florida will, what a will can and cannot do, and how to change a will.

- **How to File for Divorce in Florida** By Edward Haman, Atty., 2nd Ed., $19.95
  Explains all aspects of filing for divorce in Florida, including alimony, separation, and child support.

- **How to Modify Your Florida Divorce Judgment** By Edward Haman, Atty., $19.95
  Explains in simple language how alimony, child support, custody, and visitation can be modified.

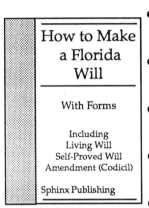

How to Make
a Florida
Will

With Forms

Including
Living Will
Self-Proved Will
Amendment (Codicil)

Sphinx Publishing

- **How to Probate an Estate in Florida** By Gudrun Nickel, Atty., $19.95
  Explains what assets must be probated, the three types of probate and how to finish the process quickly.

- **How to File for Guardianship in Florida** By Gudrun Nickel, Atty., $19.95
  Explains guardianship requirements, procedures and how to fill out the forms.

- **How to File for Adoption in Florida** By Gudrun Nickel, Atty., $19.95
  Explains court proceedings for stepchild, adult, agency and intermediary adoptions

- **How to Win in Small Claims Court in Florida** By Mark Warda, Atty. 3rd Ed., $14.95
  Explains how to proceed in filing a case, defending a case, settling a case, filing a lien and more.

- **Traffic Tickets in Florida** By John Adkins, County Judge, $14.95
  Explains your rights in traffic court including how to analyze your ticket and prepare your defense.

- **How to Change Your Name in Florida** By Mark Warda, Atty., $9.95
  Explains Florida laws regarding how to change your name legally.

- **Women's Legal Rights in Florida** By Gale Forman Collins, Atty., $19.95
  Discusses women's legal rights, how the laws protect them, and provides a comprehensive resource guide.

Business Matters

- **How to Start a Business in Florida** By Mark Warda, Atty., 3rd Ed., $16.95
  Explains how to legally open a Florida business, including laws, regulations, and ready-to-use forms.

- **How to Form a Simple Corporation in Florida** By Mark Warda, Atty., 2nd Ed., $19.95
  Explains how to register a Florida for-profit corporation, including stock certificates and corporate minutes.

- **How to Form a Nonprofit Corporation in Florida** By Sam Mackie, Atty., 2nd Ed., $14.95
  Explains how to register a Florida non-profit corporation, including how to file Articles of Incorporation

Real Estate Matters

- **Landlords' Rights and Duties in Florida** By Mark Warda, Atty., 3rd Ed., $19.95
  Explains Florida's Landlord/Tenant Laws, including how to handle evictions, abandoned property, bad checks and security deposits.

- **Real Estate Agents Rights and Duties in Florida** By Mark Warda, Atty., $14.95
  Explains the legal rights and obligations including commissions, licenses, liabilities and fraud.

- **How to File a Florida Construction Lien** (and Collect) By Barry Kalmanson, Atty., $19.95
  Explains what services and material are lienable, what the legal requirements are and who is entitled.

- **Land Trusts in Florida** By Mark Warda, Atty., 3rd Ed., $19.95
  Explains how to keep your assets secret, and avoid probate, spouses share and litigation.

Books from other Publishers

Patent It Yourself, 3rd Ed. $34.95
>Explains every step of the patent process, complete legal guide for inventors.

Plan Your Estate with a Living Trust, 2nd Ed. $19.95
>Explains estate planning for estates under $600,000, with specific instructions for preparing a living trust.

Make Your Own Living Trust $19.95
>Provides living trust forms for those with estates between $600,000 and $1,200,000.

How to Win Your Personal Injury Claim $24.95
>Explains how the insurance claim process works and how you can settle an injury claim on your own.

Elder Care: A Consumer's Guide to Choosing and Financing Long-Term Care $16.95
>Explains how to choose and pay for long-term care, alerting you to practical concerns and explaining laws.

The Living Together Kit, 6th Ed. $17.95
>Provides information on estate planning, paternity agreements, living together agreements and buying real estate.

Simple Contracts for Personal Use, 2nd Ed. $16.95
>Provides clearly written legal form contracts to: buy and sell property, borrow and lend money and more.

Stand Up to the IRS $19.95
>Explains your rights when dealing with the IRS including deductions, penalties, liens, and much more.

The Independent Paralegal's Handbook, 2nd Ed. $24.95
>Explains how to go into business helping consumers prepare their own paperwork in routine legal matters.

How to Write a Business Plan, 4th Ed. $17.95
>Explains how to write a business plan and loan package necessary to finance your business and make it work.

Legal Research, How to Find and Understand the Law, 3rd Ed. $19.95
>Provides easy-to-use, step-by-step instructions on how to find legal information.

A Legal Guide for Lesbian and Gay Couples, 6th Ed. $17.95
>A practical guide covering living together, children, medical emergencies, estate planning and more.

Sexual Harassment on the Job $14.95
>A practical guide that explains the rights of employees that are sexually harassed.

- -

Order Form

To order these publications, please fill in the information requested and send check or money order to Sphinx Publishing, PO Box 25, Clearwater, FL 34617 or call 800-226-5291.

☐ Check Enclosed   ☐ Money Order

We accept Visa, MasterCard, American Express and Discover cards.
Card number:

☐☐☐☐☐☐☐☐☐☐☐☐☐☐

Expiration date:
☐☐☐

☐ American Express   ☐ Visa
☐ MasterCard   ☐ Discover

Ship to:

Name_____
Address _____
City_____
State_____ Zip_____

To order by credit card call:

1-800-226-5291

Or fax this form to (813) 586-5088

Quantity	Title	Author	Price	Total Price

*Shipping (1-3 books) $2.50, each add'l .50¢.

Subtotal:	$_____
Sales Tax 7% (FL)	$_____
*Shipping:	$_____
Total:	$_____

_____
Signature